Praise for
BLACK JOY

"A loving homage to all members of the African diaspora who strive to preserve their personal joy at all costs . . . Poetic . . . In a nod to the significant strength and bravery of those gone before her, Lewis-Giggetts etches a stunning personal map that follows in her ancestors' footsteps and highlights their ability to take control of situational heartbreak and tragedy and make something better out of it . . . Hoping that readers embark on a quest for their own joyous preservation, she leaves us educated about the process and ready to work on the self-healing we all require . . . A simultaneously gorgeous and heartbreaking read."
—*Kirkus Reviews*, starred review

"Expanding on the author's June 2020 article about the personal and political power of laughing with her daughter, these 36 essays counter the narrative that Black life consists only of struggle and trauma."
—*The New York Times Book Review*

"The world may seek to dismantle you, but *Black Joy* . . . will piece you back together."
—*Essence*

"An essential collection on the radicalism, beauty, and necessity of Black joy to counter narratives of trauma and to celebrate wholeness and liberation."

—*Ms.* Magazine

"In an era that feels less than loving, Lewis-Giggetts reminds us that we have always been more than fighting against the forces that seek to undermine us. We have always possessed the paths to our own healing and light."

—*TheGrio*

"A piercing lyrical collection."

—*Glamour*

"For the days when you feel overwhelmed and off your game, the essays from Tracey Michae'l Lewis-Giggetts's book . . . will be the inspiration you need to remind you of the strength that you have within . . . These personal poetically written pieces are created from a place of expression that confirms the complexity of the Black experience."

—BET

"*Black Joy* meditates, and really levitates, the Black sensory and the Black sensual to stratospheric heights. Tracey Michae'l Lewis-Giggetts wields curiosity like a scalpel, revealing shards of liberation and unexpected heterotopias while loving us ferociously."

—Kiese Laymon, author of *Heavy* and *Long Division*

"There is so much conversation about 'finding joy' and 'keeping joy' as a pathway to fuller, more meaningful lives, but there is very little direction on how to do that. Tracey uses her own journey to help readers navigate the tumultuous terrain that is at the heart of holding on to our joy, especially for Black folks. So many will find themselves in Tracey's deeply self-aware, generous, and lyrical writing, but more important, so many will see that everything we have been through and everything we have are the recipe for claiming and keeping joy."

—Tarana Burke, founder of the Me Too Movement and author of *Unbound: My Story of Liberation and the Birth of the Me Too Movement*

"*Black Joy* is a necessary testimony on the magic and beauty of our capacity to live and love fully and out loud."

—Kerry Washington

"*Black Joy* is a vulnerable declaration and embodied affirmation of Black love, Black liberation, and, of course, Blackity Black joy!"

—Rachel Ricketts, activist and author of *Do Better: Spiritual Activism for Fighting and Healing from White Supremacy*

"*Black Joy* is a glorious gift to Black folks. Intimate, engrossing, and deeply resonant, Lewis-Giggetts's essays form a loving blueprint for healing and nourishing our minds and our spirits. An essential read for all of us who are trying to get free."

—Deesha Philyaw, author of *The Secret Lives of Church Ladies*, finalist for the 2020 National Book Award for Fiction

"Evocative, honest, and beautifully written, *Black Joy* is a balm to the soul."

—Bernice L. McFadden, author of *Sugar*

ALSO BY TRACEY MICHAE'L LEWIS-GIGGETTS

The Search for Susu

The Next Thing Is Joy

The Integrated Church

BLACK JOY

STORIES OF RESISTANCE, RESILIENCE, AND RESTORATION

Tracey Michae'l Lewis-Giggetts

GALLERY BOOKS

NEW YORK   LONDON   TORONTO   SYDNEY   NEW DELHI

Gallery Books
An Imprint of Simon & Schuster, Inc.
1230 Avenue of the Americas
New York, NY 10020

Some essays in this collection appeared in slightly different form in the following publications and have been published with permission:
"Dancing in the Rain and the Power of Black Joy as Resistance,"
The Washington Post, June 2020
"The Blacker the Love," *Essence*, March/April 2021
"Someday It Might Snow in April: The Healing Power of Prince"
as "Nothing Compares 2 Prince," *Dame Magazine*, April 2016
"Born to Wash Cars," MyBrownBaby.com, October 2014
"Do You Love What You Feel?" as "How Bodywork Helped Me Find
Healing from Trauma," *Catapult Magazine*, April 2020

First Gallery Books trade paperback edition November 2022

GALLERY BOOKS and colophon are registered trademarks of Simon & Schuster, Inc.

For information about special discounts for bulk purchases,
please contact Simon & Schuster Special Sales at 1-866-506-1949
or business@simonandschuster.com.

The Simon & Schuster Speakers Bureau can bring authors to your live event.
For more information or to book an event, contact the Simon & Schuster Speakers Bureau
at 1-866-248-3049 or visit our website at www.simonspeakers.com.

Manufactured in the United States of America

1 3 5 7 9 10 8 6 4 2

Library of Congress Cataloging-in-Publication Data

Names: Lewis-Giggetts, Tracey M., author.
Title: Black joy : a strategy for resistance, resilience, and restoration /
Tracey Michae'l Lewis-Giggetts.
Description: First Gallery Books hardcover edition. | New York : Gallery Books, 2022. |
Summary: "Black joy is unique and deeply rooted in the cultural experiences and expressions of Black people. It's ever-present and yet often hidden . . . Black joy has a sound." —
Provided by publisher.
Identifiers: LCCN 2021023278 (print) | LCCN 2021023279 (ebook) | ISBN
9781982176556 (hardcover) | ISBN 9781982176563 (paperback) | ISBN
9781982176570 (ebook)
Subjects: LCSH: African Americans—Psychology—Anecdotes. | African
Americans—Social conditions—Anecdotes. | Conduct of life—Anecdotes. | Joy.
Classification: LCC E185.86 .L495 2022 (print) | LCC E185.86 (ebook) |
DDC 305.896/073—dc23
LC record available at https://lccn.loc.gov/2021023278
LC ebook record available at https://lccn.loc.gov/2021023279

ISBN 978-1-9821-7655-6
ISBN 978-1-9821-7656-3 (pbk)
ISBN 978-1-9821-7657-0 (ebook)

To MaKayla:
May your joy always be limitless and liberating

There is no time for despair, no place for self-pity, no need for silence, no room for fear. We speak, we write, we do language. That is how civilizations heal.

—Toni Morrison, *The Nation*, March 23, 2015

Contents

CONTENTS

. . . *as restoration*

INTRODUCTION

Does Joy Have a Color?

Tracey, you're not very kind to yourself."

I remember those words as clearly as if it happened today. About six years ago, I came to my now former pastor for guidance. His office was draped in rich, dark browns, with black leather chairs and tasteful gold accents. I chose the sorrel leather couch that sat ominously in the middle of the room, sure that it had seen its share of tears and, maybe, sweat. The pastor perched behind a huge wooden desk that dwarfed his laptop. A globe and thick texts lined the bookshelves that took up nearly all of one wall. In hindsight, it was a lot to take in. You know how a room and place speaks to you? Tells you about its owner? Reveals the nature of its work? This office was that kind of place. And yet my mind was somewhere else. My heart was looking for something, anything, and hoping I'd find it in that office. Yes, I'd come because I needed help sorting through some specific challenges, but I also wanted to figure out a larger direction that made sense; a path that felt divine. I found myself in a place where all of the hats I was wearing, all of my identities—writer, wife, teacher, mother—were colliding into one another and I needed a kind of extraction from a reality that, frankly, I'd manufactured.

So his words startled me. "Shook" is probably more accurate.

"I don't know what you mean," I said.

I mean, I did. But who wants to concede something like that? Admittedly, this man and I would eventually butt heads on a number of things. Theology. His leadership style. And normally, I'd be ready to debate. I found myself often anticipating something off coming from him. But his simple statement couched in a conversation about my life purpose unearthed an understanding I'd chosen to not acknowledge. It hit me hard because it was true. I was not kind to myself at all.

There were a myriad of ways I could have been kind to myself—extending myself grace when a mistake was made, asking for what I want, or resting when I knew I'd been grinding too hard. This rejection of self-compassion was an interesting position to be in when you consider that I'd done all the things. I'd written about the healing power of creativity and art from a cultural standpoint. Spoken on numerous platforms about racial justice and reconciliation. Named myself a curator of Black joy through the arts. I knew how to be happy. I knew what Black joy *should* look like. I could manufacture it at the drop of a dime. But I struggled with true compassion for myself. My critiques of every minute detail (the way I looked, moved, laughed; what I enjoyed) and my work (my writing, teaching) were swift. They were harsh. I worked myself into the ground for outside valida-tion so I could feel the love and acceptance I should have been able to give myself. I had all the makings of Black joy but no recognition of it as something inherent to me, and therefore had no ability to hold it for a lifetime. Gratefully, this has changed for me. I hope it changes for many of us.

For me, the change shows up as the dancing and bed jumping I do with my nine-year-old daughter on one of our mommy-daughter trips to Atlantic City. Tapping into a purity of delight that I never before gave myself permission to experience feels like a warm hug on a cold day. Other times, it's the cheesy grin that comes across my face while watching my favorite nighttime drama. I'm a sucker for good storytelling, and choosing to enjoy a show as opposed to dissecting it is a gift. The feeling of joy in my body is intense and weighty and necessary. And, in the end, most of the moments I've taken to embrace joy and self-compassion are wrapped in my cultural understanding of who I am as a Black woman.

When attempts are made to define what liberation and equity looks like for Black people, we often hear the language of striving and collective burdens. And rightfully so. Our history is filled with the evidence that struggle and dogmatic persistence has been integral to our four-hundred-year-long freedom project. But as more and more studies reveal, the lens of struggle as the means to freedom has not come without a cost. The physical, psychological, and spiritual impact of racial trauma has often found us crossing the finish line of every battle war torn and broken from the inside out. As a writer, storyteller, and Black contemplative, I'm not sure I can ignore this for much longer—especially when there is another significant tool in our arsenal. One that not only deeply disturbs the racist systems we are trying to dismantle but also offers a direct path to healing and wholeness as we do so. That weapon is powerful and all-encompassing and necessary. That weapon is joy.

Plenty are the conversations happening right now about Black joy. The power of it. The necessity of it. The ways in which this very cultural demonstration of humanity counters mainstream narratives of Black life being solely comprised of trauma and hardship. That said, there is an aspect of Black joy that is too often overlooked and/or missing from the discourse. Mostly because it forces Black people to look inward as opposed to outward for the validation of our joy. In order for Black joy to have longevity, for it to live both alongside and beyond our movements, it must be firmly founded in self-compassion and empathy within each individual.

No doubt, we Black folks look outside ourselves for that validation for good reason. Historically, we've been dehumanized and dismissed as inferior. So through our demonstration of joy, we hope to be seen as fully human. We want our laughter to be contagious instead of treated like an audible plague. We want our dances, our food, our stories to be centered and not just commodified or colonized. And yet the most powerful thing we can do is believe all of this ourselves first. To be absolutely clear about our own humanity. To offer ourselves all the grace and benefits of the doubt that other humans receive. This is self-compassion. It requires us to create an infrastructure for the evidence and impact of Black joy in our individual lives that is rock solid before we ever seek external acknowledgment.

My inclination that day to push back hard against my pastor's candid words reflected what I already knew about myself: I had a deep desire for validation positioned within a nearly nonexistent framework of empathy and grace for myself. Even a simple compliment was often hard for me to process. Someone could say to me, "You did a great job," or, "I really liked that dress you had on," or something as simple as "I like your hair," and I'd instinctually want to add a caveat to turn that kindness into something I was not worthy of. I'd want to somehow mitigate their compliment just in case something went wrong. My inability to give myself kindness and receive it was an issue of not feeling worthy of it. So even though I hungered for these kindnesses, I had to work really hard to receive them—even from myself. It was a dynamic of longing for validation and wanting to properly process the positivity that came my way, but not being able to take it in. If this showed up in my daily life, how much more would it show up in my work? Or, in the cyber-communities where so many of us spend time? I couldn't hold properly the likes and shares I got on social media because there was no self-love sustaining me. There was no compassion for myself and my journey and so, inevitably, there was no way to hold any success.

But actually, there was. I just couldn't see it.

Being a Black woman, I had a portal to self-compassion, and ultimately joy, that I'd yet to recognize. Black joy was ever present but hidden behind and under the trauma that I wore like a badge.

Self-compassion for ourselves as individuals creates a collective self-compassion that can support the demonstrations of our joy. The historical experience of Black folks in this country made "being kind to ourselves" a challenge. We did not have time to tend to our emotional and psychological wounds while dodging the master's whip. Extending ourselves grace when we messed up wasn't an option because messing up could have meant lynching or other kinds of harm. Even today, the margin of error is very small for Black people. Benefits of the doubt are rarely extended to us and therefore we rarely extend them to ourselves.

But we must try. We must anchor our joy in self-compassion. In empathy.

Despite what many White people would like to believe, joy absolutely can have a color; a race. Black joy is unique and deeply rooted in the cultural experiences and expressions of Black people across the Diaspora. It's ever present and yet often hidden. There is a kind of laughter that only Black people recognize; one that signals more than just a "funny thing happened on the way to . . ." A laughter that unearths a salve we need in the midst of a reality that on its worst day can be insidiously paralyzing. Black joy has a sound. It moves in a particular way. It tastes like pot liquor and corn bread but, at the same time, shrimp and grits; but also *fufu* and *jollof*; and I cannot forget pumpkin spice lattes because of course we are not all the same. Blackness is not monolithic, but we know it when we see it. Its scent is subtle yet piercing. Like Great-Grandmother's talcum powder and Jean Naté, it enters the room before you do and stays long after you leave. This is why we must tap into it.

Black joy is also a strategy. The wider world dismisses and disregards it as frivolity at its peril. It is a mechanism for resistance, a method of resilience, and a master plan for restoration. That's what I hope these stories, these essays, will unpack. My aim is to make clear how it is the intentional expressions of Black joy—whether subtle or overt—that will ultimately lead to personal and collective healing for Black people, whether we conquer racism or not. I'm desperate for all my people to experience the expansiveness of healing and wholeness available to us and I think the tool to do that is something we've always had and maybe always known. When joy is Black, it is the radical demonstration of our humanity—our laughter, our ancestral mandate to keep moving in a rhythm all our own—set in a cultural context and struggle specific to our experiences as members of the African Diaspora. However, Black joy without an understanding of empathy and self-compassion is simply Black happiness, and happiness is temporary at best.

The words "joy" and "happiness" are too often used interchangeably. When we think about happiness, we think about specific moments. That time I rode the roller coaster at Six Flags. That other time I was asked out by my crush. And those are certainly worthy of being called happy moments. Happiness is the feeling in our bodies that permeates everything and tells us that "in this moment, I am pleased."

I would argue that joy, and Black joy specifically, is different. Our joy and our trauma both sit on a continuum. There isn't one or the other. There isn't a binary. The complexities of our experiences mean that our joy can live just underneath pain. In fact, it can live alongside it. It's the mother who, after experiencing the pain of childbirth, can look down at the tiny face looking up at her and feel nothing but love. Joy is that thing, as the elders used to say, "no White man can steal." It's that sense of hope; the feeling that something good can come out of the bad. It's the good part of the burnt toast. It's the donut tire that lasts longer than it should until you can get a new, regular tire. Our ancestors were well versed in Black joy even when moments of Black happiness escaped them.

And Black joy isn't happening in a vacuum. It is rooted in a deep love for who we collectively are as Black people and a willingness to vulnerably sit with ourselves and others in an act of emotional allegiance. A challenge when we consider all of the places in this world where Black people cannot sit (literally or metaphorically) safely. Licensed clinical psychologist Dr. Adia Gooden has written about Black self-compassion extensively and says in her online essay "A Case for Black Self-Compassion": "Not having safe spaces to learn to honor our pain and to be vulnerable has left us without life-giving self-compassion." She offers that many Black people feel as if we don't have time for self-compassion in light of all the work we must do to fight injustice. However, it is in the wake of that very work that we need self-compassion even more. "We need to be fighting police brutality, mass incarceration, and infringement on voting rights among other issues facing our communities. . . . I agree that these are all pressing issues," Gooden says, ". . . [but] consider what our communities will look like if they are not infused with love and compassion. Racist institutions in the US have systematically attempted to erode love and compassion in Black communities. . . . Black self-compassion is radical, it is personal and political. Black self-compassion challenges the stereotypes that we are just hard and tough, that we are not fully human."

When Black people express our joy through the lens of self-compassion, we allow ourselves to be the totality of who we are. We don't feel the need to adhere to any particular image of how our joy should manifest. We can simply be. Arguably, this is a privilege that White people often know intimately because there is no prevailing narrative to disabuse them of the awareness that they have the right to be in a space and express themselves however they see fit.

My experience with racial microaggressions and, most recently, with racial violence made the words of my pastor feel like a luxury I couldn't afford. Nevertheless, after experiencing a health crisis that made it clear just how necessary self-compassion is, I've chosen to go into emotional debt trying to build a solid foundation of grace for myself, so my small part of this massive racial reckoning we are all experiencing will endure.

When kindness, love, and empathy is directed inward as Black people, it fuels the more creative expressions of our joy while also allowing us to see ourselves in a light that doesn't often shine our way. When self-compassion is the foundation, when it is the inner well from which everything else draws, we won't feel inclined to run from our joy when it shows up. We won't tell our kids to stop dancing at the park because we don't want to scare "folks." We won't stop laughing the way we laugh, with the joy spilling out in perfect decibels, because our laughter makes White folks uncomfortable. Yes, there is a potential for violence against our bodies—we've seen that. But our joy is a weapon of resistance. Black self-compassion prioritizes our freedom. And my hope is that this book serves as one more opportunity for us to normalize our freedom and joy. When the foundation of Black joy is self-love and empathy, we can make room for all the ways our humanity shows up—good, bad, and ugly. The joy can live alongside the pain. We will be able to hold our own joy and the joy of other Black folks freely and without reservation.

In many of these essays, I talk about ancestors. Mine specifically, but also the named and unnamed whose lived experiences laid a foundation for what I understand about joy. I'm not sure one can talk about Black *anything* without considering the ways our ancestors—that great cloud of witnesses—are still speaking. As scholar Dr. Yaba Blay once said, "The idea of Black joy as a liberation strategy is an honor to our ancestors."

So much of this book is also about the relationship between the individual and the collective. In order to truly understand the myriad of forms Black joy takes, I had to personally engage with it. This was a struggle for me, as you will soon read. Writing this book taught me just how much I'd wrapped myself up in an impenetrable cloak of trauma, leaving no room or possibility for joy of any kind to enter or escape. I was telling the same stories over and over again and had become okay with being indelibly marked by my pain. These essays forced my hand, though. In order to see the potential of Black joy as a liberation strategy, I had to learn how to wield it. And that lesson was deeply embedded in my own personal healing process. I had to unpack the false narratives I'd unconsciously embraced about Blackness and its capacity for joy. If I never believed in the interconnected nature of our bodies and spirits before, there is no way I could have embarked on, much less finished, any piece you'll read here.

Here, I confronted questions I'd long neglected: What would it mean to crack open my soul and expose myself on these pages in an effort to find and immerse myself in a generational inheritance—joy—that's not talked about as much as pain or trauma? Is there a line between what I hold as truth as a Black woman and what Black folks as a collective hold as true for us as a people? I honestly don't know the answer to that last one. I mostly think that these experiences are couched in a fading gray area where overlap and incongruencies make for new realities and compelling arguments. I do know that whichever side I happen to be on—the personal or the collective—the joy narrative alone is bigger than any song, dance, movement, or isolated invention.

So no, this book isn't *just* about the Electric Slide and Afro combs and all the symbols of Black joy; all the mechanisms through which our joy finds animation. Black joy is as nuanced as the human condition. White supremacy and our struggle against it isn't the only thing that binds us as Black people. In fact, it isn't even the most interesting part of who we are. That said, the experiences of the descendants of African people (the enslaved, particularly) are convoluted at best and therefore our joy is ever intertwined with our struggle; ever integrated with the trauma wielded against us. You're surely going to have to use a different lens to witness this particular brand of joy—maybe even in these essays—but I assure you that if you're willing to see it, it's willing to be seen. Black joy is both pervasive and petty that way. No game of peekaboo here, though. Just an unwillingness to contort itself in order to become some beacon of light for the world. No, Black joy, no matter how complicated, knows its survival lies in the ability for every vessel it fills to remain free even on the inside.

...as *resistance*

A PATH TO LIBERATION
PAVED IN WHOLENESS

MAY JOY FREE YOU TO

- *Breathe deeply*
- *Love freely and with abandon*
- *Stand flat-footed in your truth*
- *Wrestle with injustice and win*
- *Return to your body*

Dancing in the Rain and the
Power of Black Joy as Resistance

> The only way to deal with an unfree world is to become
> so absolutely free that your very existence is an act of
> rebellion.
>
> —Albert Camus

The laughter that poured out of us that day was sudden and staccato much like the torrential storm that threatened to pummel my plants if we didn't close the entry to the plastic greenhouse that already sat precariously uneven in our small backyard.

"Look at me, Mommy!" she said, the Afro-puff on top of her head swelling in the winds. Her wide-mouth grin was like a checkerboard with her two missing "Dracula" teeth.

My daughter and I finally got the closure zipped when, in true eight-year-old goofball fashion, she started dancing. Her arms flailed as she did something that could only be described as a cross between the Milly Rock and the Renegade. Ordinarily my reaction would have been to say, "Girl, get your tail in this house and get those soaked clothes off!" But something shifted in me. I matched her Gen Z shenanigans with a little Gen X, old-school righteousness and hit her with a Cabbage Patch and Hammer dance combo. Then we both did something we hadn't done in a long time.

We laughed uncontrollably.

Not a few chuckles like when we see a funny meme on the internet. Not even the giggles that come when Duck mistakes some random stuffing for Bunny in *Toy Story 4*. This was a guffaw. A scream-laugh. An unearthing of all the things, known and unknown, that ailed us.

When we got back into the house, I cried. Mostly because I'd been vacillating between sorrow and rage the whole week prior and I understood what that singular moment really meant. In my mind, we were two Black girls in a backyard turning the world and White perceptions upside down with our joy. I suppose, on the surface, we both may have just needed the release. But we were also three months into a global pandemic. My daughter had not seen her friends or had a play date since March. I was wrestling with all the things most quarantined working moms had to manage. And yet, there was so much more behind my deluge of tears. I knew what our joy represented. It was its own kind of resistance. Our joy was an affront to our Trump-supporting neighbor down the street. It was an affirmation for the Black mom who lives across the street with her daughters. It was a cleansing experience for us and, in many ways, it was a demonstration of what Zora Neale Hurston once said: "Sometimes, I feel discriminated against, but it does not make me angry. It merely astonishes me. How can any deny themselves the pleasure of my company? It's beyond me." Our dancing in the rain wasn't a denial of all the storms that had moved in on Black people that week. It was a dare. An indignant stance of confidence in the midst of this malignant monsoon called systemic racism. Our laughter was a way to say "you can't steal our joy" to anyone who'd dare deny our humanity. Author and scholar Imani Perry, in her article "Racism Is Terrible. Blackness Is Not," written for *The Atlantic*, captured this feeling well: "Joy is not found in the absence of pain and suffering. It exists through it. . . . Blackness is an immense and defiant joy."

Joy as resistance isn't as much of a stretch as some might think. We constantly heard about the alleged rioting and looting happening during Black Lives Matter protests and uprisings around the country in the Summer of 2020. What we didn't hear too much about was the spontaneous breaks in protests when dancers and singers and artists took over where the chants and confrontations left off. The way the crowds stomped an insistent rhythm into the pavement felt like a Diasporic clarion call. The engagements and weddings that happened in the middle of marches were too often considered anecdotal for some but were actually intentional acts of defiance. Why else would a woman dressed in ivory satin stand before her partner, eyes wide and full with liquid love, as they said, "I do," and kiss fervently to the sounds of protestors' cheers? Choosing to express our joy loudly and without reservation is directly connected to bringing our Imago Dei (image of God) humanity front and center in the movement. And that's a necessary form of resistance because it clearly punches the lights out of the pervasive dehumanization we encounter on any and every other day.

More than even resistance, though, dancing in the rain with my sweet girl illuminated just how powerful and healing Black joy can be for Black people. It certainly was for us. That night, my baby girl slept more soundly than she had in months. I was able to quiet the panic that fills my chest when, long after the little one's bedtime, I sit at my computer and prepare to write another essay about another hashtagged brother or sister.

In the wake of George Floyd calling out for his long-passed mother as his neck was being crushed by a police officer and what I imagine was Breonna Taylor's last dream before she was shot, it's hard not to believe that the only real and lasting weapon I have as a Black mother is to circumvent these generations-long traumas with generational joy. My daughter will laugh and cry and dance as much as she likes with as much freedom as I can afford her. She will know that she can laugh and cry and dance in the sun *and* the rain.

And sure, I'm a mother. So after the laughter was over and both our hair and our hearts were drenched, I might have still said, "Girl, get your tail in this house and get those soaked clothes off!" But this time, my words were laced with some newly recovered ammunition: joy.

2

Breathe Again: A Manifesto

> Come celebrate with me
> that everyday
> something has tried to kill me
> and has failed.
>
> —Lucille Clifton

*B*reathe, Tracey.
Oh.

I quickly relax my face. My arms tingle as feeling returns to them. The pain that had begun in my forehead, crept up to the crown of my head and then back down to the nape of my neck, has diminished.

Don't forget to breathe.

I realized earlier this year that I hold my breath when I write. I have to consciously stop the flow of words and ideas and take a deep breath in order to not feel as though I'm about to pass out in the middle of whatever magnum opus I believe I'm working on. Lately, I've intentionally started taking deep breaths while writing. I do these exercises where I'll write a paragraph and then check in with myself. Write another, then check in again. Breathing full and deep while writing feels weird. Mostly because it's unfamiliar.

I'm used to shallow breathing. The environment I grew up in—globally and locally—necessitated it. Holding my breath was a way to ensure my own safety from the things happening around me. Pretending to be asleep. Pretending to not hear. Pretending to be okay. These were the ways I learned to navigate the bad things. So taking deep, loud, releasing breaths felt like a luxury I couldn't afford. Or a luxury not afforded to me. Or a luxury I never allowed myself to buy once I allegedly escaped my own terrors. And now, in my forties, I'm relearning some things. I'm having to retrain my brain, if you will, and accept that my breath is my friend. It is the source of my joy. The genesis of my healing.

I wonder if this is true for most Black folks. Clearly, there is no monolithic Black American experience, but racialized trauma is a thing. Studies and surveys from major research institutions have confirmed it. Tool kits and white papers from a myriad of sources have outlined the details. And we know that trauma of any kind has a severe impact on the body and mind. Bessel van der Kolk, renowned psychiatrist, talks about this in what some call the trauma healing bible, *The Body Keeps the Score*:

> Traumatized people chronically feel unsafe inside their bodies: The past is alive in the form of gnawing interior discomfort. Their bodies are constantly bombarded by visceral warning signs, and, in an attempt to control these processes, they often become expert at ignoring their gut feelings and in numbing awareness of what is played out inside, they learn to hide from their selves.

We also know that problems with embracing one's breath is one of many outcomes of PTSD. So I wonder if Black people, as a result of the transgenerational legacy of racial trauma and violence, are just out here holding our breaths. Taking shallow sips of air so we stay alive but do not *really* live. Because our living seems to be a threat to the White supremacist power structures that have tried, for generations, to strip away from our existence. And if so, then maybe that's why when we do experience any kind of profound joy it's so wild and full and sometimes, yes, a thundering, all-encompassing delight. In our joy, we get to breathe not with our lungs but with an untouchable, ancestral umbra. This must be the first step then. To heal. To embrace our joy we must return to the breath. Our breathing is its own resistance. An inextinguishable connection to a spirit that never dies, even if our bodies do. Because what exactly happens when Black folks as a collective start to really breathe deep? When our fear is diminished because our heart rates are stabilized and the divine life force that has been quenched in us over the last few hundred years is restored?

That's easily the most feared healing in the world.

The day after the decision came down from my hometown of Louisville, Kentucky, to not indict the officers who killed Breonna Taylor—to *not* indict them for her actual murder—I sat in meditation for a good while. For about two years, I've practiced contemplative prayer—an outgrowth of a thousands-of-years-old Christian mysticism carried out by many, including Black theologians Howard Thurman and Barbara A. Holmes, but formalized by Father Thomas Keating. One of the things we are asked to do during a session of sitting in silence is use a sacred word or phrase as a way to center ourselves. Whenever thoughts go astray, I am to gently return to the word as a way of consenting to the time of silence. The sacred word is supposed to subvert the intentions of my other thoughts and announce to my body and soul that I'm open to a deeper experience with the spirit. On this day, when once again justice was not served, my sacred word was "grace," but I struggled desperately to focus. There were emotions trapped in my body; a great sadness and overwhelming despair lurking in the corporeal systems I believe were created to keep me stable.

Because of how disoriented I felt, I shifted from my sacred word to an awareness of my breath, a useful practice borrowed from Eastern religious traditions.

Inhale.

Exhale.

Inhale.

Exhale.

It was only then I recognized the need to shift my breath, this life force within me, and move it into those places that held all my personal and collective trauma. Yes, unlike Breonna and George and a myriad of others, I still had breath in my physical body. Yes, my reality as a Black woman in America is that I did not know for how long. Every breath for a Black person is a grace in a world hell-bent on stealing our lives whether by actual execution or by the slow burn of dehumanization. But the awesome truth is, none of the villains in that oppression narrative are the givers of that grace. They have no real power over our breath even when trying to rob us of it. We must consciously continue to breathe because it is a demonstration of our defiance. Doing so

allows us to birth ourselves over and over again, into every iteration of our people's freedom journey, and *that*, I suspect, must be
terribly frustrating for our oppressors. And yes, because they are
not the ones who can give us life, they absolutely have no right to
steal it. Knowing this is the ultimate resistance. It is what Harriet
knew. It's what Nat and Fannie Lou knew.

So I made my decision. In that singular moment of stillness
I decided to not—under any condition—relinquish my breath
without a fight. My breath is my birthright but also, in light of
the journey my people have taken, a privilege. I will breathe deep
and long in the face of White supremacy. I will not abandon my
breath for any reason.

The breaths I take are connected to all the breaths taken
by those who have gone before me. I breathe and, in a way,
those who have ascended to the next phase of their journey
breathe with me. So when my breathing is shallow and my
body fills with the presence of uncertainty, I choke their air.
They recede. But when my breath is deep and steady, they are
somehow able to return to me, filling me with wisdom. Their
guidance is not hindered by my gasping. They are able to be the
witnesses they are meant to be. What does it mean to not truly
breathe more than what's needed to stay conscious? To live
in the shallow places? To fear the deep? No more, my friend.
Fullness of breath—physically and spiritually—means access
to all the resources available to us from the great beyond. It is
our passageway to joy.

There's an old saying that goes, "It's not what they call you,
but what you answer to." I solely and defiantly answer to the
name of Imago Dei, a human made in the image of God. I laugh

in the face of, dance in the presence of, anyone who would dare call me something different. Yes, my deep abiding joy is certainly a weapon used in my dissent. But I will also wield my breath like a spiritual machete against those who wish me dead, physically or otherwise.

3

The Blacker the Love

BLACK LOVE

Black don't crack love
Except on the inside love
Black as the sun's graffiti on my skin love
Black under cover love
Black in the night love
So Black I fight love

"Your slip is showing, baby."

When the elder mothers of the old Black, Baptist church of my childhood used to say this, my heart would swell. In my adolescent mind, pointing out that tiny bit of ivory lace hanging below the hem of my skirt felt like they were looking out for me. I just knew that I would never be "caught out there" because there was a line of Black women who had my back. And while I've long eschewed my slips, half joking that they were clearly weapons of patriarchy, I've never forgotten those feelings of safety and affection. Whatever the source, it felt like love.

There's something incredibly powerful about the way Black women love. It's at once sharp and pointed—edges honed by a society that too often downplays our genius or dehumanizes us altogether—while also being tender and omniscient.

We just know things. Not everything. But when it comes to matters that can't adequately be elucidated by words, we are connoisseurs of merging our knowledge (intellectual and/or street) with our passion in order to get things done. When the world rightfully celebrated Stacey Abrams for assisting in flipping the state of Georgia blue in the 2020 presidential election, every Black woman knew exactly what was at work. It was our love rising above the name-calling and defeats, not to save the nation, but to save ourselves and our babies. When Megan Thee Stallion took the *SNL* stage and demanded that the world face its denigration of Black women, we understood that also as a cry for healing. When Kamala Harris spoke directly to little Black girls in her acceptance speech, it was more than an affirmation. It was an infusion of love.

Unfortunately, when we talk about Black women and love it's too often couched in a conversation about men. It's generally relegated to the context of romantic relationships. And Black women certainly love our men—partners, sons, fathers, friends—well. But the way Black women love one another is arguably just as potent.

Our love for one another shows up at the kitchen table when we are holding the hand of our homegirl who is grieving a loss so heavy that relief can only be found in shared tears and 7 Up cake. It shows up in the fatty part of fingertips digging into tense scalps at the salon we swear by. It's in the knowing glance of the only other sister in the classroom or boardroom; the "Yaasss!" of the bartender with box braids who pours an extra shot for the squad.

Author and friend Candace Wilkins knows better than most the power of a Black woman's solidarity and care. When the delivery of her first child turned frightening, she found herself on an operating room table preparing for an emergency c-section. A doctor in the room, a Black woman, asked her if she had anything she wanted to say. Wilkins was clear: "Both me and my baby need to leave here healthy." The doctor smiled and said, "We got you."

Most of us know how to take care of one another. The qualifier of "most" is only necessary because there are some who allow fear to tamp down their empathy. But even then, the Blacker the love, the sweeter the grace. Despite one-dimensional media portrayals, most Black women know that when one of us shines, we're all lit.

There will likely come a time when our families will look less like the nuclear form designed by Western culture—if they ever have. They will hearken back to the villages of our ancestors that extended to platonic relationships. The blood memory of many Black Americans recalls this as we grew up calling our mother's friends Aunt So-and-So and claiming their children as our cousins. But I suspect we're heading toward a kind of Sankofa moment when in our looking back we know how to proceed forward. Then, the ways Black women engage with one another, the way we love on one another, will be the clear and present route to the liberation of the entire Black family.

I'll never forget enjoying a night out at a restaurant in Philly owned by a Black woman, where Black women not only served us but also were responsible for the amazing gourmet soul food menu—seafood mac and cheese and deviled eggs, anyone?—we devoured. I found myself looking into the glorious faces of three of my girlfriends—all Black—as we talked about marriages, children, and careers. Our laughter, a symphony of cackles and claps, was a balm for our own souls. When we allow it, the joy oozes out of us in lush and vibrant tones filling the room and the hearts in it. Whatever the world may see, whatever pop culture may try to poach, it's *this* particular brand of joy, this special love we save for one another, that cannot be stolen.

My curiosity about love has always unraveled me. The little Brown girl in me dangles her feet off the edge of her imagination as she tries to picture what authentic love looks like. The adult me once viewed it as fictional: an oasis that I desired to drink from but didn't really exist in the ways I always hoped for. *Maybe it is a narrative that is forever out of reach*. To even try to link love to joy felt like a paralyzing endeavor.

Does adding an adjective in front of it devalue love's core meaning? Familial love, sister love, *Black* love. Or does love illuminate in the face of such revelatory descriptors? Black love, the kind I've seen in the eyes of those church elders or in the gentle touch of my lover's hand on the base of my spine, is still one that is fraught with tension.

Black love, in many of the same ways as Black joy, has always had to fight for its existence. It is why I think the two are forever linked. It is the kind of love that, by its very presence, is an exception for some, a rebellion against all the limited definitions offered in place of it. Black love is simultaneously uncertain and unequivocal. Always anticipating the next shoe to drop. Ever waiting to catch said shoe so we can all keep walking. I imagine it feels like a partner being torn away from one's body and heart by hatred or injustice or even inner demons born from the same residue of hatred and injustice and round and round we go on the carousel of Black emotions, Black tears, and yes, on the sweetest of occasions, Black joy.

Black love seems tentative at best and yet so rich that I just want to sink my teeth into it like the decadent thing it is. Like that 7 Up cake, this time made by my nanny in her fourth-floor apartment. Made with butter she bought from the corner store. Dripping with the kind of melt-in-your-mouth flavor that only comes from an investment of time. Time way too many of us don't have. Which is why we rush. Which is why we run. Steady checking on our love. Steady checking *for* our love. Steady wanting the Blackest of love—whether from our sisters, sistahs, real mothers, church mothers, new lovers, or old—to leap inside us and fill us up. To ride the sinews of every nerve ending in our bodies, into those spaces and places that are so, so dark and so, so hidden that we don't even know where they are. We just feel them.

Some say that no matter whether the love is Black or Brown or White or like the night or like the cake I remember from childhood, it will never be filling. And that deeply disappoints me. They say that only the God of the heavens can make me whole. That it's just Jesus who can put me back together even as I am broken over and over and over again and again by life and men and women and teachers and students and those who were supposed to love me but didn't and those who did love me but couldn't show me or those who wanted to love me but didn't know how or those who chose not to love but to hurt me and hurt me bad. Those last ones? Yeah, they stuck their pain inside my pain and didn't care how much or how long I screamed, didn't care how much their words and actions copied my pain in trip-licate. Didn't care how much it would change my brain and my life forever and ever, and now these folks, these people who have never left those mahogany pews in twenty or forty or a hundred years, want to tell me that only God can heal me? That only God can lift my pain from the dark places and make me new again? They want to tell me that God is the only way and that the blood of Jesus covers me, and so they lay their hands on me dripping with dollar-store olive oil and they pray and tarry, tarry and pray, and they speak in shabbas and oboshos and even a few ashog-otahs and I walk away feeling strange because I know that they believe that God lives in their hands and that God lives in their hearts and that God can take the crowbar of the Cross and crack open my soul so that the pain can come rushing out like the tide, like waves crashing against the shore of my salvation, and yes, in one singular instant, in one moment of clarity, in one side-eye-filled second of revelation, I realize that they are right.

They are right.

They are right.

But not in the way they think. Not in the way they believe.

They don't know that I've seen God do his cracking open in the shimmering eyes of my nine-year-old as she touches the sky on her trampoline. They don't know that I've heard God's heal-ing in the pure laughter of my sister friends at the Black-owned restaurant around the way. And yes, they don't know that I've felt the salvation of God in the slip lined with lace as I touched the hem of my own garment.

They are right.

And they don't know.

4

Conjuring Angels

You lifted me. And not in the way that some would consider affirming. You never held me up in admiration or placed me on a pedestal solely because I was "such a pretty little girl" or "smart as a whip."

No, you lifted me like a petty thief lifts costume jewelry off the spinning carousel at a discount store. You were like those teenagers I saw once who filled up their '92 Honda Civic with gas and sped away without paying. Only you weren't a teenager and there was nothing costume or discount about what you stole from me. Gosh, I wish I'd known that then.

You, sir, were full-grown.

I'm curious. What gave you license to do what you did? And what did you end up doing with my innocence? Because you seemed to need it pretty damn bad. When those who would have or should have protected me were held captive by silence, you seemed inexplicably desperate. Only a few years in this world, I didn't have the words for it. Couldn't articulate what I clearly recognize now as your attempt to extract my soul from my body one touch at a time.

Still, I wonder if you actually saw the angel at my door that last time. The one with the pointy hat and long robe. What exactly did they say to you?

For such a long time, there were so many questions that came after. Like, what about the other days? Where was my angel before? Why didn't someone come and save me?

But then I remembered my prayer.

You see, some of the answers we little Black girls seek are forever lost in the winds of memory or imagination. Why did Mommy cook baked chicken with no skin on my fifth birthday when she knew I liked fried fish sticks and fries? How did Michael Jackson turn into a zombie so damn fast in his "Thriller" video?

But there are certainly other things exposed with time. The day before that night, when I sat in the sun wanting the light to never end, when I sank low with dread of what the darkness would hold, my secret power was revealed.

I was a conjurer.

I learned that if I raised my voice high above my fears it would reach the heavens. And it was this power that delivered to me the courage to tell. It was this power that taught me how to effectively fold into myself so no matter what you did, you couldn't take everything. It was this power that helped me find all my pieces and replace them with better ones that fit just fine. And it is this power that allows my angels and me to, even now, crush the demons of your creation that periodically try to rise up and break me.

Oh yes, you lifted me, all right. And for a little while, I was broken because of it. But after much work, I'm strong. Not super-strong. No *S* on my chest; never get sad or anxious because Black girls don't do that kind of thing, strong. Just regular, ordinary, been through the fire but came out like pure gold, strong.

But you're not getting any passes, though. There's not a single point available to you just because what you wrought in my life didn't kill me. The outcome, the victory, is solely mine and my angel's to own.

5

I've Got Dreams to Remember, Granny

UN VIAGGIO IN CINQUE PARTI

1.

My granny called me Petey. I can hear her raspy elongation of the *e* vowel in my head even now.

"How's my sweet Peeeeetey?"

It simultaneously unravels and soothes my soul to hear those words pierce the dimensions of heaven and earth; the rivers of gold she crossed more than eleven years ago.

The story goes that the name stuck because my pint-sized self would run around her house screaming over and over again, "For Pete's sake, Granny!" I don't know where I got it. I suppose it was one of those phrases that just tasted good to the toddler palate. I'm sure the staccato sharpness of "Pete" tickled my little fancy and sounded like something an adult would respond to with laughter and kisses. And so I added the phrase to my growing repertoire of phrases like "Mommy said" and "I want applesauce!"

I spoke very early and much of that can be attributed to my granny. She was my sitter for the first three years of my life while my mom went to work, and she did not do baby talk. She spoke to me with the same tone and tenor and mostly the same language she used with Miss Violet, one of her uber-fly girlfriends who came over to smoke cigarettes and drink beer with her. Miss Violet was a beautiful woman whose face stayed "beat to the gods," as makeup artists say today. Granny and Miss Violet would cackle about men and there was usually one in particular who would occupy at least a portion of their conversations— Victor Newman. Victor was the ruthlessly vicious yet debonair lead character on the soap opera *The Young and the Restless*. Yes, Victor and Marvin (Gaye) and Smokey (Robinson) were always in the mix with the ordinary Oscars and regular Richards.

I, at once, knew all this and I didn't. I was two, maybe three years old, so my witness is probably not the best. Do I really even know what my granny and her girlfriends were talking about? Maybe not. But I did the math and she was thirty-nine when I was born—several years younger than I am now—so I'm quite sure they weren't talking about Mighty Mouse or the Romper Room. And when blood memory jumps wildly in my veins whenever I hear a Sam Cooke or Supremes or Aretha Franklin record, when Otis Redding croons "I've Got Dreams to Remember," I know for sure they weren't.

I mostly just recall the laughter. The way they'd unleash whoops and hollers that would soar through the room and wrap me up in joy. I'm grown now, so of course I know the back stories. The divorces and wayward children; the job losses and gains. Granny's house was filled with a generationally familiar prepackaged happiness. The laughter, whether from a kiki with her girls or a raucous win at backgammon, was never a surprise. It was a known glee. Granny was neither spontaneous nor vulnerable then. Mostly because life wouldn't allow her to be. Bouts with depression had long snatched Granny's breeze from under her wings. She chose her own sovereignty and preferred her happy to be one of her own design. Even better if it came in a bottle or pill or mink coat. Her concept of freedom and happiness would always be the glamorous shade of red that offered a quick pop of color against the stark drabness of life. It could never, ever be the whole picture.

But back then, to my three-year-old heart, her laughter just sounded like love and safety. Her presence energized my little body; every moment creating neural pathways my soul would need to hold on to when life went left. The evenings watching *Star Trek* on the couch, tucked under her arm. The days watching her paint the ceramic figurines she'd spun and carved herself. My three-year-old self sucking on the fatty gristle of the T-bone steaks she made every week. The smell of Sterling beer and Virginia Slims cigarettes. The coffee mugs with cherry red lipstick stains and the clanking of silver hoop earrings and bangles. Right there in her Bent Creek apartment, I first felt the power of a kind of joy, even if sporadic and disjointed, that fights off demons with skill and style. I was Viola Brown's grandchild and she loved me.

2.

There are things I wish I could say to her. Words that form in my gut and with age and courage have found their way to the edge of the cosmos. I can only hope that she can hear them on these pages. That their sound reverberates across the universe to whatever place of wonder allows her spirit to now run free.

My granny wasn't the Big Mama type of grandmother. The kind characterized on television and in movies as a gray-haired, Bible-toting Black woman dressed in a caftan with a fresh pot of collard greens and corn bread on the stove no matter the day or hour you showed up at her door. That was more my great-grandmother, Ora Lee Lopez. Granny wouldn't have been caught dead in a caftan or muumuu, and while she was a fantastic cook, she preferred to experiment with gourmet dishes like coq au vin or something that required a risotto and not the usual white rice that came in ten-pound bags.

And you'd better not even dare try to show up at her house unannounced. She was liable to hear you knocking and remain seated on her couch reading *Vogue* or a James Patterson novel, completely unbothered and unmoved by your unsolicited presence.

She was what other members of our family called bourgie and low-key proud of it.

After leaving Louisville not too long after I was born, Granny—always reinventing herself—traveled the world for over fifteen years as a caregiver and tutor for high-profile families and those who had children with special needs. She worked for eighties fabric designer Jay Yang, novelist Erica Jong, and cared for Mrs. Christian Grey herself, Dakota Johnson, the daughter of actors Don Johnson and Melanie Griffith. Granny spent a bulk of that time working for the Forbes family and loved to tell us about that one time she read Walter Cronkite for filth at a fancy dinner.

By 1983, she was spending time in France and Italy as she traveled with one of the families that employed her. Granny would always bring back wonderful gifts from her adventures. Purses and bags; T-shirts and other trinkets. But she went all out with her belated eighth-birthday gift to me. She knew I was a huge Michael Jackson fan. I'm sure my mom told her that the walls of my room were papered in his image; from the yellow vest and single Jheri curl tendril hanging delicately from his forehead to the edgier picture of him in a denim jacket and finger-waved sideburns. All the way across an ocean and two continents, Granny sent me the most amazing gift: an Italian leather Michael Jackson jacket similar to the one he wore in the "Beat It" video.

I was aflush with joy. I couldn't believe I had this coveted jacket right in my hands. Sure, the studs on the shoulders looked a little different from the one he wore in the video, but the bright orange leather felt like I'd slathered butter on my arms. I couldn't wait to wear it to school.

I wish I could tell my granny how much that jacket meant to me. Of course I told her, "Thank you." "You're welcome, my Petey," she said from a half-dozen time zones away. But I want her to feel how, even now, my heart races with excitement at the specificity of her adoration of me. This urgency I feel has its roots in guilt. Because I only wore that jacket one time. When I walked into my third-grade classroom, face filled with pride and pre-tween swagger, the other kids verbally ripped me to shreds.

"Ew, that don't even look like the real Michael Jackson jacket."

"Stop lying! Your mama bought that on Fourth Street."

It never occurred to me, Granny, that it was envy at the

source of those assaults. I was eight and carrying the weight of a secret—my sexual abuse—that had already begun its work of dismantling what I understood about my self-worth. My eight-year-old self thought the jacket, infused with your love, could make up the difference. Sometimes I do wish it held that kind of enchantment. But it was, in fact, just expensive Italian leather. Known to move a grown person to spend a mortgage payment on shoes. But never able to summon acceptance for the little girl who longed for *that* above anything. That little girl couldn't see that the love driving the purchase of the jacket and the deep joy it initially sparked was enough; she was enough.

She wants you to know that she understands that now.

3.

Tonight I am curled up in the sweet spot of our new bed. We've bought homes and whatnot, but it is *this* bed I recognize as a truly grown-up investment. Who knew there were mattresses that cost the same as a small used car? Yet here I am. Tucked in the equivalent of a 2010 Ford Focus; nestled in fourteen inches of luxurious organic cotton and latex and pushing buttons on a smart remote to find my perfect sleep setting. I feel an overwhelming sense of security settling in the sinews of muscles I've been holding tight for more than thirty-five years. Something is releasing. The tears started about five minutes ago and now they are soaking my face and neck. My body remembers.

I've never felt safe in a bed before today. Scratch that. There's been only one other time I've felt safe in a bed.

While the career of later years took her around the world, my granny eventually settled down in a condo in Cape May, New Jersey. This kept her in proximity to New York City, where the families she worked for lived, but still allowed her to have her own space. One year, I think I was thirteen, we drove from Kentucky to Virginia Beach to visit family and then made our way across the monster also known as the Chesapeake Bay Bridge to visit Granny. I danced on the deck of the Cape May Ferry as soon as I could see the port up ahead. *Petey is coming! Petey is coming!*

After spending our days at Wildwood Beach, my family would eat a grand meal and then make our way to our respective sleeping quarters. I'd hit the grandbaby jackpot because I got to sleep in the room with Granny. Right up on her big queen mattress, I tucked my body next to her long, lean frame and slept more soundly than I probably had in years. I also nearly suffocated on the cigarette smoke. Granny was still chain-smoking her Pall Mall cigarettes, and my eyes stayed red for nearly two weeks after we left. But it didn't matter to me. I gladly inhaled her secondhand smoke in exchange for her firsthand asylum.

An unprotected child will sleep in a cloud of toxic smoke if it means she will feel the warmth and security of a body she has absolutely no doubt would shank a nigga if they tried to hurt her. My granny would surely shank a nigga for her Petey.

More than thirty years later, that feeling consumes me as my body reminds me that I do know what safety feels like. It may have been hard to come by in this life of mine, but this glimpse into the kind of peace that's been available to me in fits and starts is exactly the kind of reckoning I need. No shanks necessary.

4.

Today my soul aches for you. Today is the day you left us all those years ago. The day when your spirit took flight. The day when you escaped the weights that held you, the pain that enflamed you. The Tuesday before you soared, you'd said that you just wanted to hear my voice. You said that you were going to be fine. You were right, I suppose. But there is one thing that I do not understand.

You were ready to go, but the stories were not. Why did you take your stories with you? The ones about being born in the Jim Crow South. The ones about falling in love with my grandfather and giving birth to my mother at eighteen. The ones about your mother and your mother's mother, both of whom I'd never met.

I needed the lessons and language to fill out my own narrative, but now they only exist in the ether. And the holes left behind feel so vast. Like gaps in the lexicon of my life. And days like today, when I long to sit under your bosom, to brush your charcoal hair, to eat the gourmet soul food you'd make just to flex both your Virginian and Parisian journeys, I wish for it more than ever. Help me please to find your stories in the air. Send them back to me from the heavens. I want to free myself. I want to teach my baby girl—oh, you would have loved that juicy one—to know what freedom feels like in her skin.

5.

By 2004, Granny was just trying to live. The cancer had spread. Metastasized, the doctors said. But she was still trying to live.

She read at least seven books a week. Every Saturday, she carried a suitcase down to the library bookmobile that came to the senior citizens apartment building she lived in. She had a man. Some cool, biscuit brown septuagenarian who lived three floors up in her building. She had her hair. Despite rounds of chemo and radiation, it was as stubborn as she was and never fell out.

My theology was different back then. The first time that it looked like she wouldn't make it (and there were many times—stubborn, I told you), I became preoccupied with making sure my granny was saved. I'd say things like, "Oh, I just couldn't live with myself if I didn't witness to Granny and she went to hell." Cue the Oscar music.

It sounds beyond self-absorbed to imagine me saying something like that now. Because of course, God would totally allow the salvation of a woman to hang in the balance because of the non-action of her twentysomething grandchild who was living six hours away in Chicago at the time and was even herself not quite as saved as she wanted her granny to be.

There was no dissonance for me, though, at the time. I wasn't the one dying. Not as quickly anyway.

"Did you get my letter?" I asked her on one of my visits. I'd written her a letter outlining the "Roman Road for Salvation" and had even given her a script to pray.

"Yes."

The term "side-eye" wasn't part of the pop-culture lexicon in 1999, but it was most certainly a thing.

"What did you think?"

This was another way of me asking if she'd prayed the prayer. Today my deconstructed faith doesn't rely much on certainty as

33

a necessity for spiritual acuity, but back then it was the corner-
stone of everything I believed. I needed to hear her say that she'd
said the actual words. The "burdens of my heart" would only be
relieved with that confirmation.

"Girl, I've been knowing about that."

Um, okay?

I didn't know what that meant. I couldn't even tell if it was an
opening for further conversation or a complete shutdown.

For Pete's sake, Granny.

I decided, though, to not press it. Granny was *grown* grown.
She'd seen more God in her life than I'd dare to pontificate on.
Born in the post-Depression South, coming of age at the dawn of
the civil rights movement, and a former military wife two times
over, my granny had been delivered over and over and over again
from every inner and outer war imaginable. And although her life
may not have been replete with all the love and joy she desired,
all she deserved, she certainly gave what she had to me. Her
liberation—in whatever form—was never my responsibility, but
mine is certainly an echo of every hope she sought but couldn't
speak. Her reinventions—as unpredictable as they might have
been—paved the way for my own resistance.

6

Leaving Louisville

I was born in what used to be Methodist Evangelical Hospital on East Broadway in Louisville, Kentucky. From ninth
grade until I graduated from high school, I participated in the
Black Achievers program at the historic YMCA on Chestnut
Street. Like most Black folks I knew, I celebrated the Kentucky
Derby with barbecues, fish fries, and, when I'd sneak home
from college, the grand block party thrown by the Screaming
Eagles Motorcycle Club. We rode up and down Broadway in
the souped-up cars of that one cousin or that one guy we grew
up with who had the booming speaker box hanging out of his
hatchback trunk. I'm old enough to remember when hanging out
at White Castle—because what was gluten?—or Robben's Roost
Skating Rink was a significant highlight of most Black teen life in
Jefferson County. Louisville is where my story began. It's where
my past took shape and it's the place where my future stories will
always and forever be linked. Many in my family still live there
and, in retrospect, I suppose a piece of my heart remains lodged

somewhere between Hurstbourne Parkway and Shawnee Park. It's my hometown.

Yet after graduating from the University of Kentucky in 1996, I couldn't wait to drive as far away from the Bluegrass State as I possibly could. I packed up a rented Budget cargo van with borrowed furniture from my granny and, with $300 in my pocket, drove myself to the South Side of Chicago, vowing never to return.

So far, I have not.

As I get older, my reasons for this position become more nuanced. I now recognize every memory I have of living in Louisville as being both painful and glorious. It is a city I treasure while still holding it at arm's length. Nevertheless, so much of my perspective is rooted in the city's complicated history around race.

As a child, it's hard to pinpoint what you are sensing when you encounter what the grown-ups around you know to be racism. Kicking my Mary Janes wildly in the grocery cart and singing "Jesus Loves Me" at the top of my lungs, I remember the snide looks of the Winn-Dixie or Buy-Low cashiers as my mother put her food on the belt. But of course, I couldn't yet fathom what those looks meant . . . I think I remember the mixture of anger and sadness that blanketed my mother's face as she watched the cashiers watch her. But I couldn't yet understand why she was upset.

As young as seven years old, there was always something that made me feel uncomfortable when I had to be in all-White spaces. And because of my parents' choice to live in the East End, being in all-White spaces was and is very common. While I'm aware that this is slowly changing, it doesn't seem to be fast enough, nor is gentrification ever an answer to anything. I always half joke with my mom that, after living in cities like Chicago, Philadelphia, and New York, where it rarely happens, I always feel strange coming home and going to restaurants because it's entirely possible to still be the only Black people in the building. Joke aside, growing up there, I could never completely articulate why I felt a subtle, under-the-radar terror in certain places. It always seemed like White folks could go from friend to nigger in 2.6 seconds. And, worse, until recently, no one ever really talked about it. I'm not sure we even had the language for the microaggressions or anti-Black racism we experienced back then. It was normalized.

This was just what it meant to grow up Black in Kentucky.

As many already know, Kentucky's place in the story of race in America is informed by its position as a border state— politically divided over slavery during the Civil War. It was a nebulous place where White supremacy reigned despite its efforts of neutrality. A state that prided itself on being a place where Lincoln and the Union troops could set up camp but also adopted as its state song a pro-slavery anthem that announced, "The head must bow and the back will have to bend, wherever the darkies may go." Crossing the Ohio River to the North was a beacon of freedom for many enslaved Africans escaping the chattel slavery of the Deep South. It meant that they had reached what they thought would be the last stop on a train of terror. In one sense, if one could get out of Kentucky, then one could possibly be free.

I identify with that.

And I really thought it would be different up north.

I know there is a group of scholars and writers who have tried to make the Great Migration and Black folks moving from the South to the North or West some kind of indictment of those who stayed behind. The Great Migration, as much as it is a model for liberation, should never be weaponized against those who chose to stay and build a life; to endure the overt terrors and stand their ground on land drenched in their ancestors'—yes, even their own—blood. These critics attempt to create a binary that essentially implies that the ones who left to go north or west were smarter than the ones who stayed. As one who left, I can unequivocally say, they are as wrong as two left feet—ironically, something my southern great-grandmother would say.

In the early years after moving, I certainly *believed* that going north would offer me greater opportunities. That going to the "big city" would somehow refine and define me in ways that staying back home in Kentucky would not. But what I did not consider was that, when I moved to Chicago and later New Jersey and Philadelphia, I was taking my Kentucky sensibilities with me. I would also soon learn the shape-shifting nature of racism; a characteristic that allows it to show up as one thing in the South and another in the North but remain equally violent.

The systems up north, by and large, are just as undergirded by White supremacy as those in the South. And, in fact, the layers go much deeper when you add the intersection of class. As I said, I didn't move to Chicago with a bunch of money. I had a job, a lease, and three hundred bucks. Whatever money my parents had stayed right there with them in Kentucky. So at twenty-two, in my search for "something else" up north, I often came face-to-face with a more visceral, taunting form of the very things I left behind.

I had my main gig working as a recruiter for a management consulting firm, but because I needed to make money fast, I took a part-time job as a telemarketer. It was a small outfit that would work on various campaigns calling folks all over the metro Chicago area. Sometimes we were calling folks asking for political donations and other times we'd be asked to push some product or another. In 1997, telemarketing calls were pervasive, so I quickly learned how to detach from anything true about myself in order to make the deal.

I was on a phone call with someone when, in the middle of my script, the man immediately homed in on my accent.

"Where are you from, missy?" he said.

Cringe.

"Well, I'm in Chicago."

"Oh, you're not from Chicago. Where are you originally from?"

Just get the deal.

"Kentucky. Would you like to . . . ?"

". . . Ah, okay. Okay. That figures."

His next two questions totally threw me.

"You're Black, aren't you?"

I didn't say anything. Which I assume he took as confirmation.

"Do you have on shoes?"

Wait, what?

I tried to make sense of it. I was young and it didn't click yet. First of all, I'd said I was in Chicago. Second of all, even if I were in Kentucky, why would he think I didn't have shoes on? And what did me "sounding Black" have to do with any of it?

Obviously, I didn't get the deal.

Deep down, I knew the implication even if I didn't want to admit it. Even if I still wanted to believe that things would be different in the big city. For that man, being from the South (Kentucky was considered the South to folks in Chicago even if many people still consider it the Midwest) meant I was backward. Being Black and from the South damn near made me primitive, I suppose. It was eye-opening to say the least. A stark realization that racism and classism, while different, was still racism and classism.

I'm a lot wiser now. A bit longer in the tooth. And though I still live up north, I've starred in many scenes of "Close Encounters of the White Racist Kind" that let me know the racism I've faced here is not any better than the kind experienced down south. It's different. Maybe it's more subtle. Maybe. It's definitely hidden under the façade of progressive posturing that many liberal Whites don here. And I've settled for it, not because I'm smarter, but because my stomach is different. Having now lived more years out of the South than I lived in it, I've simply built a tolerance for and accepted this *kind* of racism. And yet, even as I hope for better in my city of residence, I still long for better in my hometown. I still hope that maybe change will happen somewhere. If not here, maybe there?

Imagine then what it felt like for me to sit in my office in Pennsylvania and hear the attorney general of Kentucky announce the results of the grand jury investigation into the officers responsible for killing Breonna Taylor. My blood ran hot, then cold. Tears

I'd determined would not fall drenched my cheeks. While sorrow and rage filled me, there was no surprise. Of course they would not directly indict these officers for her murder. *It's still Louisville.* The city's fake neutrality that allowed the walls of Taylor's neighbors to be more valuable than her Black body was predictable. And yet there was still the sinking feeling that comes when you realize that the place that raised you hasn't changed much. It also confirmed so much of what I've always known about Kentucky. It's a place deeply invested in "good ol' boy" and "happy Negro" politics. And it's gone on for far too long. Case in point: Mitch McConnell has been a part of the Kentucky political tapestry since I was two.

I'm forty-five.

As someone who writes about social justice issues, for many years I'd begun to develop a strange immunity to all the stories about police brutality and racial violence. Maybe it was a typical PTSD response to triggers: Shut down. Don't let it trigger you. Rail against the injustice, but don't feel too much, because another is coming.

Then it was my turn. On October 24, 2018, my family was changed forever. Right here, in *my old Kentucky home*, my elder cousin Vickie Lee Jones drove to her neighborhood Kroger grocery to pick up some things. She would never make it home. Cousin Vickie was shot dead in the parking lot by Gregory Alan Bush, who, according to the implications of a witness, decided to end my cousin's life because she was Black. This not only hit home for me because it was my family and I grew up in J-Town, the suburb of Louisville where this happened. This also shredded my insides because, like never before, I had to reconcile that what my parents and family always said was true—*this is just the way it is here.*

I wish I could say that in the years since she was killed I've been able to fully maintain my hope. If I'm honest, being from Kentucky has always meant that hope was this ever-elusive carrot held out by the people who love me. But that carrot is regularly snatched away at the news of lynchings called suicides across the country. It's snatched away with every report of a police officer's use of excessive force. It was snatched away that day as I listened to the Breonna Taylor decision and learned that, again, Black lives don't matter.

My husband has asked me a few times if I would consider moving back to Kentucky. When I hear his question, I get that same weird feeling down in my gut. I would love to be closer to family; reconnect with friends from high school and college. And Lord knows I'm grateful for the people on the ground there who are fighting the good fight. No place in this country is a racial utopia, *and* living there still feels like walking directly into the line of fire or diving headfirst into the pit. From the personal to the political, growing up in Louisville taught me that I'm never really safe. A lesson every Black person learns no matter where we live, I suppose. The Breonna Taylor decision just confirmed it.

One of the hardest things that we will ever have to reconcile individually and collectively is the fact that sometimes choosing joy means leaving a place that no longer serves you.

Choosing joy might mean leaving someone who is no longer able to hold space for all that you are. For me, finding joy in my life, or putting myself on the journey toward finding joy, meant leaving the city of my birth. It also meant returning two decades later to intentionally make peace with it. I love Louisville. Deeply. In hindsight, I know I was running from more than just the city when I left. I was running away from all the ways that the city had negatively informed me. I wasn't yet willing to reconcile that with all the ways that the city had actually positively shaped me too. All the ways the city had done a good service to me. But nevertheless, my particular path, my journey, called for leaving, and I'm fine with that.

I don't know if I would ever have been able to find joy in the way that I needed to find it had I stayed. And for that reason alone, the risk was worth it. And so I think we have to sometimes reckon with the notion that there are places and people and things in our lives that will require us to remove ourselves from them in order for us to grow. It doesn't mean that we won't return. It doesn't mean that we won't come back to those people, places, or things. It just means that in order for us to ground ourselves and find our footing, we may have to go. I've since learned that joy is an inside job. For a season, it might be okay to chase it. But at some point, we have to cultivate it on the inside so that no place—hometown or not—has the power to steal joy from us.

It doesn't feel good to know that my home city and state will be immortalized in rap songs and protest pictures not for the wondrous way my gold-toothed aunties slam down the dominoes during the Derby or flick their cards down in a spirited game of Tonk. Not for the way the vanilla ice cream tastes so sweet and goes down so smooth in the mouths of plaited, Brown, baby girls and little Brown boys with fresh fades at the dairy spot in Chickasaw Park. Not for Big Red soda or Indi's rib tips or KingFish or the Belvedere. No, *the 'Ville* will only be found in the verses about Breonna's body being riddled with bullets by a system that said her walls were more victimized than she was.

And yet those same gold-toothed aunties don't stop playing. They don't stop eating rib tips that make a mess of their Sunday 'fits. And every person who took to the streets in Breonna's name still has a choice as to whether that city, the state, this country, or those bullets will steal from them the only thing they/we truly own—their joy.

7

Smells like Blackness

AN EXERCISE IN MONOLITHIC IMAGININGS

The rusty musk of the fake gold door knocker earrings. A hint of nineties adolescent naïveté in overalls with cities airbrushed across the butt. Phrases like "old enough to know the game, young enough to play it" trailing up the thighs.

The pungent soilishness of cooking collard greens. The sweet sweat of Double-Dutching divas as ropes graze the concrete. The enticing smolder of macaroni and cheddar cheese and Monterey Jack cheese and any other kind of cheese—especially the corner piece with the crust. The heady fervor of Auntie beating cassava into *fufu.*

The warm, earthy heat of our collective breath when we "Aye!" on the fifth turn of the Electric Slide. The tartness of top lips as faces turn up in appreciation of her hippy, sexy, dance-hall wind.

The piquant of ambition that hovers over the booth as he or she or they drop bars in the studio. Matter of fact, it's in the damp and dogged stamina of hip-hop. The curative balm of soul music. The defiant stew of Trap and Screw.

It's the holy lexicon that idles on our tongues. The scent of the *jive turkey* or *fresh* or *dope* or, at least round 'bout Philly way, the *jawn*. The full-lunged drags we take of stale and ancient books whose pages reveal the blazing brilliance of Baldwin and Morrison and Hurston; of Lorde and Walker.

Moist hands clapping in the Black Baptist or Pentecostal Holiness or Church of God in Christ or African Methodist Episcopal churches of our childhoods. Olive oil and sweaty brows of preachers and prophets and priests matching healing herbs and oils from the earth with the savory spirit(s) in the sky.

The incense of kitchen table secret keeping. Salon tea spilling. The hotfooted hustling of water on the street; T-shirts at the concert; noni juice and prepaid legal services; CDs at the barbershop; rap debuts, mixed tapes, or first novels from trunks.

Wrap dresses and head wraps hold the aura of our nimbleness. Our duality is like a rose: both beautiful and thorny to the touch. Like our corporate blue suits with kente handkerchiefs or pink and green, or blue and white, or blue and gold, or red and white lapel pins.

The thick, slick anointing of Blue Magic grease being spread in the parts on Nana's pre-pressed hair. The familiar rich comfort of a heavy-handed smear of cocoa butter or shea butter or Vaseline, in a pinch, on the faces of Brown babies. The Jean Naté of Big Ma at Lil' Man's graduation.

We are overtaken by the aroma of community when we walk into the salon or the barbershop or the basement of Aunt So-and-So's house on such and such street. Our own colonies where familiar are the fumes of bald fades and bobs—asymmetric or otherwise—and Afros and twist-outs and cornrows and locks or locs or dreadlocks or dreads. Of the Anita Baker or the Halle Berry or the Sade or the T-Boz with the creamy crack of Dark and Lovely, Motions, or Mizani. The charred bouquet greeting of the Dominican press. The incense of innovation that lingers over the Poetic Justice braids or the roller wraps or the roller sets or the finger waves or the finger scrunchies or the crochet braids. The subtle notes of accessibility with the Virgin or the Yaki or the Remy; the lace fronts with the braid down or the leave out.

The crispness in the way we go "awf" in our mastery of the arts and sports and science and math and any other door we kick down. The bite of our bounce back game. The wispy side-eyes at White male foolishness on the job. The rancid realization of White folks who have for too long mistaken their mediocrity for superiority.

The dewy old-but-new-again fragrance of marching in the streets, of rising up in the streets, of lying down in the streets, of the "No Justice, No Peace" in these streets.

The peculiar and natural delight of our laughter and joy. The peculiar and natural intimacy of our sorrow. The peculiar and natural urgency of our rage.

The delicate balance of honoring the struggle but standing true in the candy-coated awareness that we are and have been the originators of nearly every major American and/or global cultural moment, musical genre, socio-political movement, pop culture fascination, and artistic innovation.

There's more than just a zest to this. There's levels. Melanin pheromones give off something both ingenuously human and astonishingly divine. Inhale the way we move. Exhale any definitive notions of who we are. We're never outdone. Never putrid, never spoiled. Always an exquisite mix of both sharp and misty virtues.

Like good and bad Black. Like hot and cold Black. Like near and far Black. Like everything and nothing Black.

We are.

8

We've Always Known

BLACK SOMATIC EXPERIENCING

The body, not the thinking brain, is where we experience most of our pain, pleasure, and joy, and where we
process most of what happens to us. It is also where we
do most of our healing, including our emotional and
psychological healing. And it is where we experience
resilience and a sense of flow.

> —Resmaa Menakem, *My Grandmother's Hands:*
> *Racialized Trauma and the Pathway to*
> *Mending Our Hearts and Bodies*

Sit down.
    My body first tried to speak to me in hushed tones.
Finish your water.
Maybe you should take a walk?
    A whisper that would force the hairs on the back of my neck
to stand at attention. If I noticed.
Say no. It's not worth it, she advises.

Say yes. You need the help.

A nudge of memory. A scent of suggestion. She'd call out to me from underneath the weight of my own and others' expectations. When that didn't work, she decided on a more direct approach. A headache here. A mite of vertigo there. Pain that wouldn't lay me out but could temporarily halt any forward movement until I remembered to breathe deep and long.

But like a wayward lover, I'd always go back to my old ways. The push past reasonable boundaries to garner me praise. And so she had to take more drastic measures.

July 5, 2019

Last night. An episode. Felt like someone shoved my brain. Then I felt off. Not quite dizzy, but like everything was heavy. Like I was walking through mud. And that thing in my chest. Whatever it was felt like something moving up my chest. The constant tingling in my hands and feet. Now it's off and on. The scariest part? Losing my thoughts. Not being able to think. Not knowing what to say next even though I could hear myself talking to the paramedic. Weird.

That day in 2019 was the beginning of a nine-month battle with an unnamed illness. I'd had minor issues before, but there was a dramatic shift in my health that July. I spent most days in the bed or in my garden when I wasn't going from doctor to doctor getting numerous tests done. I even took a medical leave of absence from teaching. Every day I wondered if I was going to die.

To live in my body is to recognize the ever-present tweaks in my gut. The bubble threatening to burst. It's always wondering if the next word or action from an unsuspecting or even suspecting person will be the thing that turns this around for the better or completely pierces the tenderness in my abdomen causing me to burst into a million pieces.

To live here in this body means an awareness of burgeoning tears just behind my eyes. Of a roaming tightness in my muscles. Of a heavy chest taking shallow and choppy breaths when danger is near and even when, in reality, it isn't.

To live here in this body also means a mind in constant override mode. Deciding to press through pain and exhaustion. On a mission of ambition but mostly of survival. There's actually nothing mundane or regular about the way my body works, the way it chooses life every minute when maybe death could be easier. It's a marvel. A miracle. But I don't allow myself to treat it as such on most days. Because learning the language of my own body would mean acknowledging the toil it endures. Sometimes at my own hand.

More than I care to admit, I treat my body like a frenemy. Like a loyal friend who is treated like trash because I never learned how to love her. She's always there. But I don't always trust her. I make up stories about why she's doing what she does. Most of those stories are rooted in half-truths, what I need to tell myself in order to survive the day. My legs hurt because of fibromyalgia—true. They also hurt because I'm weak—not true. They hurt because I didn't exercise—half-true. Or because I work too much—half-true. That back-and-forth makes it challenging to dig past the obvious—throbbing muscles and deep aches—and find the source. Trauma trapped in muscles. A memory hiding in my knees. Because how do you explain that? "Oh, there's my abuse acting up again"? The hard truths aren't acceptable. And while yearning to be seen and understood by anyone, about anything, *shouldn't* necessarily be a priority when one is trying to manage chronic pain and heal from trauma, it sometimes feels like the only normality I have left. And so I grasp it tight. I hold it until my knuckles turn white because letting go will hurt too damn much.

During that "downtime," the hunger to know what was going on with my body was real. I felt like I was trapped in a shell that would only allow me a few hours of energy and relative painlessness a day. So I devoured books and articles about the relationship between PTSD and physical illness. I tried every healing modality available to me. I prayed. I cried. And then I researched some more.

I learned about the real ways disease is fueled by trauma. I could finally connect the dots between the PTSD I already lived with, the breakneck speed at which I was working, the racial violence that had recently touched my family, and my body's complete breakdown. But before I could throw a pity party and cry out, "Why me?" I shifted my reading and conversations to the ways in which the body can also restore itself. The way movement and meditation can shift the nervous system back into a healing state.

And it all sounded incredibly familiar.

Everything I was uncovering was made real in the stories I'd hear of late-night country juke joints where the swaggy twists and lusty grinding of bodies to the rhythm of their blues gave an inexplicable relief to a people who held back their grief out of fear of White terror and disregard. It was made real in my memories of church ladies rocking back and forth, front to back, in the Black churches of my childhood. The way they stomped a hole in the floor and screamed out in pure elation or agony depending on the Sunday. I've come to realize that they instinctually knew how to move that trauma out of their bodies. We gravitated to things like dance and sports and music, not just because that's what White folks allowed us access to, not just because we were forced at one point to entertain them, but because, in a way, it was our saving grace. It was physiologically the way we healed ourselves. And maybe that's how we were able to not only survive with our humanity intact but also retain our joy.

> *My true believers, fare ye well,*
> *Fare ye well, fare ye well,*
> *Fare ye well, by de grace of God,*
> *For I'm going home.*

These spirituals, supported by both hand claps and moans, reveal to me an innate understanding by my ancestors of the power our bodies have to heal. Not to mention that rhythmic sound and movement was a resistance all its own for the enslaved. One that flew under the radar and turned calls to Jesus into codified messages of escape and soothing reassurances to those who needed to live another day. The hand dances of the enslaved African who cried out, "Hambone, Hambone, where you been?" might have also been a way to experience the power of compassionate touch without getting in trouble. Something I didn't know when they were handed down to me in the form of the hand games of my own childhood: "Down, down, baby, down by the roller coaster. Sweet, sweet, baby . . ."

There's something about the old hymns, though. The way those mothers of the church would sway to a beat provided by Sunday shoes and wooden canes. It's like they knew. They didn't have the fancy language, the academic jargon, for it. They didn't do any research on somatic experiencing and how moving the body in certain ways can help alter how trauma functions in the body or move it out entirely. They didn't study polyvagal theory or read *The Body Keeps the Score*, so they didn't tell folks that the quivering of their lips or the rocking side to side was creating bilateral stimulation, which would later be proven to calm a person experiencing trauma-related anxiety.

They just had the song. The rhythm. The meditation that came in the form of a repeated chorus or ad lib. The call-and-response that allowed them not only to talk back but also to talk it out. And in talking it out, even in vague "Hallelujahs" or dubious "Let him use yas," they didn't have to hold it. The pew was the canvas that could hold whatever they left there.

They knew.

They knew because many of the same ones rocking in that church spent the night before rocking to Bobby Blue Bland or Prince or Sly Stone or Jimi Hendrix. I imagine them hearing these men rip the scales on their guitars and feeling another kind of liberty, the kind that comes in the here and now and not the great by-and-by. Every pluck a release. Every chord a clemency. I consider this in the same way I regard my first encounters with hip-hop. That day when I was in third grade, when every kid in our apartment complex brought out their cardboard boxes and we attempted to pop, lock, and spin on our backs like Shabba Doo and Turbo did in *Breakin' 2: Electric Boogaloo*. I think I tried to spin my soul free out there. The movement that came along with hip-hop in its earliest, purest forms was a kind of emancipation. The beat that was like acupuncture for my spirit. It pricked me so good and ever so slightly and all the bad things I was holding, the things that went bump in the night, came pouring out of my awkward nine-year-old limbs.

I knew.

Then something happened to me somewhere along the way and I forgot.

As a child, I remember feeling like I was bigger than my body. I remember feeling like I could do anything. I would stand in the bathroom naked, singing and dancing to Janet Jackson. I could literally see myself on the stage dancing next to her. I would imagine myself all different places—on the moon even. There was a feeling that nothing could hold me back. I think there's something in the human spirit, something in the sinews of our muscles and in that space in our gut, that allows us to feel uncontainable when we are willing to embrace it.

As a kid, maybe three or four, I remember hanging out with my aunt who was only eleven years older than me. She always took me swimming at the pool in our apartment complex. As soon as we'd get in, she'd wrap my tiny arms around her neck and secure my body to her back as she would swim back and forth on the deepest side of the pool. Most kids are only comfortable in three or four feet of water if they can't swim. They tend to stay in the shallow end. But I somehow knew that as long as I held on to her neck, I didn't have to be afraid. Even if I were to let go, I had no notion of what it meant to drown, so I wasn't really afraid of it. I only knew that I loved the feeling of being one with her and the water, floating and riding along as she dipped and splashed. Nothing could hurt me, I thought. The joy of that moment was found in my indescribable sense of being safe.

Somewhere along the way, I lost that. The world reveals itself as unsafe and you can't turn back from what you have seen . . . or what you know. This is especially true for many Black folks. Life teaches us that in fact, you cannot do everything and no, you cannot be just anything. Or, if you want to do or be anything, it is going to require sacrifices that you may not have the capacity to make in the moment. My body longs again for that feeling of being uncontainable. I want to bust down the doors, break the chains, and remove the limits from myself and my people. I want to feel what it's like to go to the absolute brink of my imagination. I'm trying every day to regain and reclaim that sense of myself. That sense of being bigger than even my body can hold.

When I think about my "triggers" and the subsequent responses of my body—panic attacks, pain, headaches—it's often easy to get so frustrated. To wonder why I "can't get things under control." I keep thinking about how much I don't want what White folks do to me and/or my people to have so much power over me. But all of my irritation never changed a thing.

There is another strategy available to us. One that, with consistency, can not only restore us but also frustrate the hell out of those who seek to destroy us. It's gratitude. I've begun to specifically thank my body for the hard work it puts in to keep me safe. Because guess what? My great-grandmothers all somehow knew that it was the body that would serve me when everything else was out of my control. In a demonstration of the ultimate creativity, God designed these bodies intricately to be able to sense danger and to sound the alarm when it doesn't feel safe. God also created our bodies to be able to heal ourselves or return to "baseline" when danger has passed. It's the trauma/traumatic event we experience that messes all that up. Not the body. It's the trauma that has thrown off our sensors, causing our bodies to react as if we are in danger when we aren't. The trauma is what causes my body to react as if I'm nine years old and it's still 1985 and not 2021. Too many of us are trying to solely fix our bodies without processing and working through the trauma. I would submit that we flip that thinking. Process the trauma and use the body to help us heal.

I've begun to stop blaming my body for doing what it was created to do. Sis has put in work for almost forty-six years. She been knowing what to do. We been doing this.

9

Joy in the Details

I thought it was clean. My mom told me to "go clean your room," and when I did, it looked pretty good to me. I'd put my books away. Folded my clothes. Made up my bed. What more did she want?

She wanted the details.

Mom is a meticulous cleaner. She's the type of person who gets giddy over a new steaming vacuum or the latest edition of the Swiffer. When I was a teenager, that was a constant battle between us. Because washing dishes was never a gender-neutral chore in my home—in eighteen years, I don't remember my brother ever touching a bottle of Dawn—Mom and I would butt heads regularly on whether that tiny, nearly microscopic dot on the back of a plate was a remnant of her casserole or not. At the end of the day, she wasn't impressed with things just looking "put away." She wanted the dust gone. She wanted me to get at that woodwork. The venetian mini-blinds that hung in my room needed every slat cleaned.

"What is all this in your drawers?"

[Insert me, blankly looking off into the sunset.]

I was never really good at details.

I was always a big-picture person. *What is the end goal? What are we trying to accomplish? You want my room to look clean? Well, that's what I'll give you. Who cares about the crevices?*

Apparently Mom did. And a whole bunch of other folks too.

Over time, I learned to execute the details. I worked as an editor for some time and the very nature of that job required me to stop and check the details. It required me to slow down and pace myself. There were systems and style guides that needed to be followed. Accuracy was extremely important. But the resistance was never far away. I was always more interested in the outcomes. I wanted to get to the goal. And even today, as a writer, I'm very Dorothy Parker–ish. I dislike writing but love having written.

As a result of being this way, though, I often made quick and not-so-great decisions. This came up recently as my husband and I began looking for a home. The very first house we toured was amazing. There were some minor issues, but the fact that we agreed that it was perfect for us meant that, if we could, I wanted to put an offer on it immediately. So I went home and tried to accelerate the financing process. I sent paperwork within nearly seconds of our mortgage processor's request. Because I'd already moved in my head, I spent time looking for furniture and thinking about where I'd place my garden.

"Wait. Why are you rushing?" my husband said.

"Because . . ."

The truth was difficult to articulate. The eight-year-old in me truly believed that if we didn't act on this perfect house, there would be no more perfect houses for us. So when the home went under contract before we could get our financing in order—because mortgage companies (especially the ones who ask Black folks for a written explanation of the coffee we bought in '04) are not the ones to be rushed—all the half-truths I believed were affirmed. I was so triggered by the experience. Once again, doing all the steps, working the details, meant not getting what I wanted. I should have done what I always did. Got ahead of it. In the past this has looked like taking the first thing—the first job, first man, first house—that came along. I stuffed down what I didn't like because the idea of losing what I did like was too awful.

My resistance to process, to details, is a safety mechanism. I know that now. The feeling of something being taken away from me was something I faced quite a bit as a child. Whether it was not getting the jeans I wanted when we went school shopping or being sent away for a year because I finally told someone about the sexual abuse inflicted upon me, having to wait or "go through the steps" or "take it one day at a time" inspires a fear in me. It's the reason why I've pushed and rushed and often manufactured outcomes. It's the fear that the goal will never be reached. Fear that the end result will never be acquired.

For some, having systems and steps is useful. They create safety in that you can believe that if you do 1, 2, and 3, then inevitably 4 is next. For me, however, there were so many times that I did 1 and 2, expecting 3, and it never came. Life never showed me that waiting brought optimal results, and so having systems and steps actually triggers anxiety. I often figure I need to get to 4 as fast as I can because who knows what will happen while I'm lollygagging at 2 and 3. What I had to learn the hard way was that 2 and 3 was where I cultivated the joy I needed to sustain myself at 4.

I wonder if this happens collectively? If some of us Black folks take the first crumb given by a system that has never demonstrated care for us. We want the crumb. Deserve it even. The crumb is absolutely a victory. But we deserve so much more too. The problem is, waiting for better feels like a game of chicken. Our trauma has taught us to take what we can get and run with it . . . maybe even literally. Yes, our "magic" is found in our ability to turn most things into art, beauty, resilience, et cetera. But when we demand more, when we are willing to walk out a process that is hard and seemingly fruitless, we gain more.

See: Montgomery Bus Boycott. I imagine that while they endured the hardship of walking everywhere . . . they also laughed and talked about Uncle Jack cutting the fool the night before. While walking or carpooling, they were able to have Baby Girl and Lil' Man recite their times tables over and over. In the midst of choosing to wait . . . joy may have flourished, which, in turn, shored up their resolve. Being allowed to sit in the back of the bus was crumbs compared to what we really deserved.

And I'm clear that the bus boycott is a microcosm of a macrocosm. Some might argue that simply being able to sit anywhere on a bus is a crumb compared to a systemic overhaul, the diversifying the hiring of drivers, et cetera. I won't argue that. The truth is . . . it was a step. It was part of a larger process that understood that jumping directly to the end goal wasn't the best use of our collective effort or the way to preserve our ability to see and be joy in this midst of pain. Whether this was conscious or not on the part of our leaders is irrelevant. Our ancestors had ensured us this as their legacy. It was in our blood.

But I still get why some Black folks now find themselves feeling resistant to waiting for all the steps to play out in order for us to acquire justice and equality. To some extent, the racial violence we've seen in the last few years felt inevitable. It feels like the result of our waiting too long for a system that is functioning exactly as it was designed to right itself. We aspire to peace and equal opportunity. We aspire to a dismantling of White supremacy, the system that ultimately facilitates our dehumanization. But there's sometimes this sense that if we don't skip or hurry along all the processes—if we choose instead to savor all the individual and collective healing that can happen in the interim—then the things we aspire to, the things we desire, will simply go away. My friend, filmmaker Christina Faith, puts it like this: "Sometimes it's easier to shield ourselves from the disappointment rather than lean into the hope." In the area of social justice, the stakes are higher and our systems have proven not to care. It makes sense then that some of us feel an urgency to the extent that we say, "I'll sleep when I'm dead," or, "I'll go to therapy after we get this bill passed."

I see this showing up at the relational level too. Taking time to build relationships with White folks is complicated because of the details. If I go into one for whatever reason, I want to know up front where they stand because if I take the time to organically learn who they are, where they come from, and why I might be drawn to their friendship, I'm likely to uncover motivations or a history that will shatter any possibility of relationship in the long run. Hence, I enter every engagement with a White person with an internal—and sometimes external—side-eye. I don't want to see the details. Because my experience has taught me that the details, the crevices where their true beliefs live, will always reveal something that makes the end result impossible to come to fruition.

This also shows up in my work. I know that if I focus solely on getting the job, the deal, or the contract, then I can save myself from being devastated by the details of why they hired me in the first place. I know there's a large segment of White folks who believe that Black people *want* to be chosen for an opportunity solely for the color of our skin. They've created a narrative in their minds—born from a deep belief in our inherent inferiority—that any effort to diversify a space is simply a way for us to steal something we don't deserve. The truth is, most Black folks enter these spaces way more qualified than their White counterparts—simply because we've always had to be better in order to even arrive at consideration. We know that once we are given access, once a door has been knocked down, we will thrive because it's likely that we've been preparing for that very thing all along and for much longer. So when an opportunity is given to us because we will help an organization meet the "quota" or meet the goals of its diversity initiatives, we often focus on getting in the door and being what we've always been: excellent. If we thought too hard about the details—all the years we worked without the recognition we deserved, all the sacrifices of mind, body, and spirit we made, and all those who are still doing so—it would be so much harder to excel.

Looking at details brings the truth closer. As much as I have loved certainty, there have been some things I just didn't want to know. It's the way I've survived.

For Black folks, I think there are one of two ways we've lived through our experiences. Some of us keep the hard truths, the reality, at a distance so we are able to keep our eyes on the prize, so to speak. Others of us keep the truth up close and personal. In order to move through the day with most of their sanity, they need to stay acutely aware of the details. They need to be able to touch the truth, turn it over in their hands, and never ever forget it—even if that means forgoing any long-term advancement for themselves. These two approaches to survival have been necessary. They are a sign of our resilience, our ability to do whatever needs to be done in order to get where we need to go.

But lately I keep coming back to this question: What does joy require of us? I wonder if there is a way to live in the tension of these two methods of survival so that we not *only* endure or elevate but also do so with our hearts and minds and bodies intact. The absence of the latter being a clear consequence when we skip the steps of soul care and relational integrity on our way to social justice or some narrowly defined notion of success. What if we are able to see the truth, the details, up close and personal, are willing to face our processes and move through whatever healing steps are necessary, while also holding the hard reality of what racism produces loosely so that it all has the opportunity to evolve us?

Embracing joy and the healing that comes with it opens us up regardless. If you are like me and tend to refuse to see the details, joy in the form of being present opens you up to the possibility that your hope does not have to be in vain. It allows for you to arrive at your 4 whole and not ragged from dodging the steps. If you are the type of person who clinches your reality desperately as a way to remain safe and sure and sane, joy can loosen your grip just enough that your heart and mind can dream again.

Either way, the dishes get clean, justice comes, and we arrive at our destinies healed and whole.

10

This Is Me

I rarely watch a film twice. In fact, I can count on maybe one or two hands films I've watched more than once. And this is usually by accident. A function of said film being aired on television and me just happening to be in the room. This isn't a judgment against films, of course. I love them. Have even produced a few. I suppose it's more about not wanting to know what comes next in the story. I revel in the anticipation that watching something I've never seen before offers. My body will ache to know whether the girl will realize that it was the boy she loved all along and whether he will get to the radio studio in time to profess his love. Tiny hairs on the back of my neck try to touch the sun when I'm trying to figure out if the villain will finally see the error of his ways and join forces with the hero to save the world.

This is the direct opposite of how I approach my life. I relive every story and narrative. The record of my life plays on a loop, which would not be so bad if my inclination weren't to emphasize the parts filled with discomfort and strife. It's never a good thing to wade in the struggle to the exclusion of everything else—including joy. I wouldn't figure that out, though, until I was forty-two and I finally recalled what joy felt like in my body while watching an episode of the TV series *This Is Us*.

I wish I could tell you what it was. The thing that Randall or Kate or Kevin said that triggered this response in me. To this day, I do not know and, as you might have guessed, I'm not about to watch it again to figure it out. All I know is something happened with one of the characters at the height of the second act and my body began to tingle.

What in the world?

Then a warmth overcame me and all I wanted to do was smile. Hard. I mean, a full-out cheese-fest with no one in the room.

So I did it. I cheesed. And then I laughed. Hard. It started low like Miz Sofia at the dinner table in the final scenes of *The Color Purple*. It ended like the psycho lady in a horror flick.

I'm fairly sure there was nothing funny about the episode.

I'm officially losing it.

Then I remembered that my therapist had recently asked me what joy felt like in my body. I couldn't answer her at the time. I had no idea. I spent so many years—decades—wading in my pain that I didn't know how to identify joy when it showed up.

Of course I'd experienced joy before. I know joy was there when I held my baby girl for the first time. But my heart was cloudy with fear and anxiety. I couldn't access the fullness of it. I couldn't name it. Joy came in fits and sputters for me. I'm not sure I ever really knew what it felt like in my body. I never took the time to be still long enough to allow joy to settle into my soul's crevices. Life didn't allow for that. I had to keep moving.

I had to keep it pushing, as the elders used to say. I thought if I sat still and allowed myself to truly feel then I'd "get caught slipping" and anything good that came out of it would vanish. So I ignored the sensation. Pushed it down.

It was much easier to recognize and categorize what my pain felt like. To tell that story over and over again. To build a life and a career around my alleged vulnerability because people who are hurt are drawn to people who are hurt. And what a wonderful way to get the attention and validation I so desperately lacked, to use my writing as a way to trauma-bond, right?

Naw.

At one point in my life, I'd become obsessed with being seen. Trauma taught me very early that the way to be loved and valued and protected was to perform. In my mind, I wasn't inherently worthy of those things. I attached my worth to knowing all the answers in class or being celebrated as "supersmart" by the elders at church or being "talked up" because of my degrees or my accomplishments. Social media, with all its likes and follows, became a problem for my psyche as people began to respond—good and bad—to my writing. It had even gotten to the point where even simple things—yes, like dancing and singing with my daughter in the rain—had a small element of performance to them. *Maybe if they see me with her, they'll know I'm a good mom.* I'm not proud of this, but I'm also clear I wasn't born this way. Life is the ultimate artist shaping and forging your identity out of the circumstances of your birth and your environment. I wrestled for a long time with what it meant to be wholly southern, shadily midwestern, and undeniably and irrefutably a Black woman. What it meant to struggle with every one of those identities in some way, shape, or form. And that showed up in the work.

But that can only last for so long. Any attempt to grow, to evolve, shined a light on the desperation at the source of my emphasis on my pain and struggle. Though never my intention, it started to feel like I was using my trauma to gain validation. Who am I without the trauma identity? Who are we as Black folks, particularly in America, outside of the trauma of our arrival and the continued impact of racism?

I do not mean to invalidate my experiences or denigrate my earlier work. I eventually learned that Facebook has nothing on God's algorithm. Me and my work would be seen when it was time. Plus, my story would have gaping holes if the hard places I've traversed were left out. Much in the same way Black folks must never stop talking about the impact and residue of the transatlantic slave trade on our present and future experiences because it has informed the plight of multiple generations of Black folks who came after.

What I am saying, I suppose, is that my trauma isn't the only chapters in the book of my life. There are chapters that have left me bursting with light. Which, by the way, is exactly what joy feels like in my body. Like my stomach and chest are so full of sparkling light and it will ooze through my pores like fresh water from a rusty well. There's a tremble in my hands. Tears threaten to escape as they tingle the corners of my eyes. I usually start to rock because somehow the movement eases the sweet overwhelm. There goes that soothing bilateral stimulation. It's why rocking a baby can calm their wailing. The back-and-forth movement hearkens back to the womb and swathes us in safety. And I was feeling all of that watching a one-hour drama on television.

This is it! I finally found it!

I was finally feeling joy and it was thrilling.

It had nothing to do with the show (sorry, Beth and Randall). It had everything to do with the storytelling. I get high off a good story, told well. It moves me in a way that not much else does. And I think I've been chasing that hit all my life. At least since Maria's story time on *Sesame Street* or Sherri Chessen's mesmerizing voice on *Romper Room*. Or maybe it was the way Heavy D said, "I'm a quick rhyme shooter, rap rookie recruiter, I always say could, never ever say coulda," in "Mr. Big Stuff" and I got my entire life. It was the storytelling in the show that triggered the rivers of joy in me. I was just free enough to finally feel it.

The liberated Black body (which is inextricably linked to a Black mind and Black soul) is able to feel not just the pain inflicted on it, but also joy in all its iterations. We can sit deep in it and allow it to overtake us without fear of the many repercussions that exist. This is the ultimate resistance.

What does it mean to hold so much joy in my body, the same body seen as inferior, as inconsequential, as unacceptable in this world?

Maybe it is the ultimate evidence of God. That there is something bigger and greater that allows my laughter to block the lash, my rhythm to wreck the warden, and my voice to wrap itself around the grave and squeeze every bit of life out of a seemingly perpetual and generational death.

That, by definition, is Black power. Joy is a power that can't be stolen. It's what allows us to fly away while still remaining grounded. It travels incognito in the deoxy- and the ribo- and the nucleic-, and the acid. Every twist of its helix is lined in a spiritual valor that has baffled the colonizer from the beginning.

Here's the real revelation in all this: I'm just as courageous rocking back and forth on my couch watching *This Is Us* immersed in a kind of story ecstasy as I was spilling my pain on the page and pontificating about my struggle. My power lies in the merging of both strategies because it unveils my authentic self—the biggest threat to any system that tries to unravel me.

11

E-40 Taught Me

Here comes the top notch, ooh, ooh, ooh . . .

When Suga-T popped on the screen rocking a roller set bob and that satin pink turtleneck, you couldn't tell me it wasn't the greatest thing ever. I'd prance around my dorm room like I too was the only female rapper in E-40's Bay Area rap crew called The Click. After her verse, filled with metaphor and simile and other devices I'd just begun to explore in my own writing, E-40 would hit me with his trademark voice—a cross between the sounds Mario and Luigi would make when they'd fall off a cliff in the *Super Mario Bros.* video game and the telemarketers who would call the house trying to sell us time-shares.

I be more hipper than a hippopotamus,
get off in your head like a neurologist

I loved it all.

Mostly because I've always been drawn to song and rhythms. I love the way music pierces my soul. The way lyrics tell me a story that allows me to climb inside the mind of the songwriter. I get a feeling of freedom when I sing or dance or listen to music. When I was younger, it was so much more than escape. It was a way to imagine myself different and separate from the reality I lived in. It allowed me to move in whatever way I deemed fit. Through song, I could see myself differently.

She is the little Brown girl, plaited hair set as a crown on her little head thrown back, as she sings with her whole heart, "Jesus loves me, this I know," to anyone who crosses the path of her cart at the grocery store. Decibel levels be damned.

The same girl hums the tune to the seventies edition of the Mickey Mouse show as she plays with her favorite tea set in the tiny two-bedroom apartment she shares with her then-single mom. M-O-U-S-E-EEEEEEEEEEEEE.

A big girl now, she hovers comically close to the silver boom box, finger poised over the pause button so she can halt the flow of Heavy D on his rendition of the Jean Knight classic "Mr. Big Stuff" and write every single word and inflection change down. An excellent study for her own bid at the next middle school, lunchroom cipher.

The girl, a teenager now, joins several singing groups, which, yes, are maybe just a group of girls with big dreams like her, getting together and harmonizing to their favorite TLC or En Vogue songs. There is no Joe Jackson or Mathew Knowles to propel them, but their passions are clear.

She's grown now. Brown girl running from club to club in Chicago and New York. Running from rhythm to rhythm as she percolates herself into a stupor to the sound of Green Velvet or Frankie Knuckles. Still drawn to rhythmic dreams she can't quite catch.

Talent shows and choir rehearsals, and later dance clubs and Napster, were my safe places. The Prince and New Edition albums, the high school marching band practices, the need for quarter notes and eighth notes and sixteenth notes to create everything from an adagio to allegro rhythm in my own heart, were real. I soared far away in the songs. And even when my insecurities took over and I didn't sing as loud or as well as others, I still got to fly and that mattered more to me than anything. The music sent me to a place of quiet comfort; of sanity and security. The music had the capacity to make me feel in a way that was safe. Every shift of my embouchure on my clarinet or saxophone, every wild Cabbage Patch or Wop I wielded for the elders egging the kids on at the family reunion, granted me the power to respond to my emotional pain with a melody.

This is still true today. Even as I write this, it's clear that the memories attached to lyrics and songs don't have as many hard edges. The songs I love—even the problematic ones—don't cut me. E-40's "Captain Save a Hoe" doesn't wound me because at seventeen I truly and fiercely wanted to be saved. My reality compelled my spirit to cry out for protection and the song, as corny and fun as it was, was a buffer for the pain I felt for not having it. Of course I would later learn that salvation never happens outside myself, that no man can save me. But in the meantime, these songs were a salve wrapped in possibility. Every refrain, a softer landing place. It was liberating.

The best songs are the ones that incessantly repeat a word or phrase in the chorus or bridge. They become like meditations. They aren't necessarily the most creative or impactful or whatever measure we have this month for great music. "Best," in this context, just means "most effective." These songs make their case without trying too hard. They tell us exactly what they want us to feel and what they want us to do as a result of that feeling:

I move, you move, just like that.
I can see your halo, halo, halo
Put all your hands where my eyes can see

So I suppose the truth is, I listened to artists like E-40 and others not necessarily because I was taken with their talent or mesmerized by their message. Maybe it was less about the lyrics and rhythms and more about who I saw in the proverbial mirror when I listened, sang, or danced to them.

When Mary J. Blige crooned the first "You" in her debut single, "You Remind Me," I lost my mind. I was nearly sixteen and starting my first job at the Burger King down the street from my home. The five-to-nine shift was so "all the way live" we'd nicknamed it the BK Lounge. We'd have a blast serving customers and talking crazy to one another behind the counter. As someone who would close the store often, I couldn't wait until we locked the doors because sometimes we were allowed to blast music while cleaning the dining room.

When Mary sang, "The way you walk and the way you talk and . . ." I would sing along to my mop-turned-microphone. I saw myself in the flyest gear and rocking the hottest hairstyles. I would dip and tip around the linoleum floor with all the swag and confidence I thought I could never have outside my own imagination, until Mary showed me what it looked like on a regular Black girl with nothing but heart and ambition on her side.

This music allowed me to imagine myself in ways I didn't know how to be outside my imagination. When I sang and rapped to the first single from Mary's first album, *What's the 411?*, I saw myself bold and fearless. *That* Tracey could quickly and succinctly clap back at a dude who stepped out of line, whereas in real life either the words would be stuck in my throat, pushing down into the shame that already lived in my gut, or I'd spew rage like fire trying to burn the guy and everything around him down to the ground. Mary gave me gray area. My imaginary clapbacks, while setting boundaries (language I'd yet to learn), were still attractive. In my mind, as I glided across the gold and red Burger King floor, I was wearing Mary's sexy tomboy style and not the navy blue and maroon uniform. Her style was mine and both were unmatched. There wasn't much I'd discovered about myself in real life yet that was as effortless. And yes, as a church girl, I loved the gospel music I sang in the choir and listened to when my parents were watching. There was a different elevation, a different salvation altogether, happening there. But, if I'm honest, E-40 and Mary taught me things, gave me something, that The Winans couldn't.

Again, this wasn't escapism. That oversimplifies and ultimately diminishes the beauty of what these songs did for me. I wasn't necessarily trying to *not* be myself. I was imagining the me I could be. The same but also different. Trying to conceptualize the possibilities of a life outside of what lay before me. Outside of these songs, joy came in staccato moments. I often held on too tightly to the terrors that haunted my dreams and stripped me of my self-worth. But with my eyes closed, a nod of my head, and a near-ancestral connection to the music escaping my voice, I could resist what life was showing me. I was more.

Black folks have always imagined being more when our reality said different. We've used a myriad of things to capture that feeling, but the most powerful conduit has been our art. It's been said that we lose ourselves in music or literature or art. I disagree. I think we find ourselves there. Our humanity is forced to live in our imaginations as a kind of holding cell, until we can make them realities through our fight. Just like sixteen-year-old Tracey, I don't think Black folks create to escape. We create to reimagine. To blaze a path toward reinvention when our creations are stolen and commodified. To *be* when we are told that our only purpose is to *do*. I've often tried to envision what it might have been like to be a Black teenager in the South of the 1960s, listening to Nina Simone pour out her soul on the record "Mississippi Goddam":

Alabama's gotten me so upset, Tennessee made me lose my rest,
and everybody knows about Mississippi Goddam

I sit my soul in the skin of that child. I sit in this song, in this era, finally hearing someone say what I heard my mama and grandmama say at night when they thought I wasn't listening. Finally hearing someone who felt what I felt but who was also bold enough to speak truth to power and call out those who did the evil I likely saw each and every day. I imagine in my mind becoming Nina, dark and lovely, fearless and sanguine, telling racist White folks who had the audacity to tell civil rights leaders to "go slow" to go to hell.

In this new skin, I hold space for the little sisters who came before. The ones chanting in the fields and the ones moaning in the house. The ones in the juke joints and the Jack and Jill debutante balls. The followers of Booker T. and the Talented Tenth of DuBois. And simultaneously, across time and space, I embody the little sisters who come after. The ones who will scream, "Oooh, ladies first!" with Queen Latifah in defiance of misogynoir. The ones who will stand down the National Guard in flowing maxi dresses with faces of steel. And yes, the ones who danced to Mary J. Blige within a Burger King dining room.

Through these songs, all of us can access the kind of courage that, in real life, feels as far off as the freedom we hope to see one day.

12

Tiny Revolutions

Tiny resistances were a kind of healing . . .
—Robert Jones, Jr., *The Prophets*

Looking at my daughter is often like looking in a mirror. If I ever wanted to know what the free version of myself would be like, it's there in front of me every single day. Admittedly though, one of our biggest challenges in parenting has come from her wanting to challenge all boundaries and us feeling like we need to hold firm to them. Us knowing that for a little Black girl (hell, even for a big Black woman) boundaries are sometimes very necessary. But I am also very protective of her freedom; the way that she moves through the world with this confident sense of self and fearlessness. I want to make sure that even as we're teaching her about the reality of the world she lives in and how to respect boundaries, we're also leaving room for that free part of herself to roam. I do not want to quench her spirit.

So when she was heading to kindergarten, we did all the things that parents do when trying to figure out the best place to educate our children. We considered public schools. We also researched the parochial ones in the area. And, though certainly a privileged option, we also visited the private schools nearby. Academics were important, but racial diversity also factored tremendously in our decision. We wanted to make sure that she was in an environment where there were people who looked like her, as well as people from all different cultures and backgrounds. And we thought that we had found that place. It was a small private school that seemed like a great place where she could be herself and grow.

As she was beginning to learn how to socialize and play with other children, as well as interact in the classroom, we began getting feedback that basically amounted to: your daughter is too much. The language was coded. They acknowledged her intelligence but would also talk about her excessive questions and assertiveness on the playground.

At first, my instinct was the instinct of my mother and my mother's mother: *I know you ain't going out here acting a fool at school. You need to know how to act, girl.*

We did the things that parents do. We said, "Okay, you've got to stop doing that. You've got to listen. You've got to share. Try not to talk so much." And this, by itself, wasn't a bad thing. There were absolutely parts of her behavior that we needed to help her with. But she was also five. And extroverted. Like every other child in the class, she was learning.

What kept bugging me was this pushing of the narrative that she was "too much" for these other children and, in particular, for the teachers. That her personality was too big. Because that really was the underlying message the school was giving us. And that was problematic for me, mostly because it was familiar. Little Black girls with big hair and big smiles and big ideas are told all the time to dim their light. They are told very early on that their way of seeing the world is not worth consideration. People become uncomfortable with them because of what they see in them. They tell these little truth tellers who know exactly what they want and, in some cases, are able to articulate why they want it that their dreams and desires are too large for the world they live in.

It was familiar because I was a little Black girl once whose mother was told that I raised my hand or talked too much; that I had too many questions. And it's taken many decades and many more dollars of therapy to find my way out of those lies.

Not my kid.

I was torn for the longest time. But after a few years of her being at that school, dealing with bullying, and being labeled as the kid who was "too much" or "too weird" and her having to carry that label from one grade to the next, despite growing and learning and changing, I had to finally put my foot down.

Here's what you're not going to do.

I said, "Yes, there are things we will work on at home, but what you will not do is make my child feel like she's an outsider. You will not make her feel that her differences somehow make her unworthy of the same type of attention or engagement with her peers and with the adults who stand in authority over her." And when things didn't change, we found a wonderful school that embraced the fullness of who she is and who she was becoming.

Maybe that doesn't seem like a big deal. You might be thinking that this is something every parent might do. And maybe it is. But as a Black mama, I know the stakes are higher. As a Black mama who had this baby later in life, one who's already wrestling with her own healing journeys while trying to do her best to make sure her child doesn't become the next leg in some relay of generational burdens, this was my revolt. It was my way of saying that the buck stops here. My advocacy for my child was my tiny revolution, my little protest. It was me saying that with *this* particular child, in *this* school and in *this* year, the kind of adultification and diminishment that happens to Black girls will not happen. Not on my watch.

As Robert Jones, Jr., implies in the quote at the beginning of this essay, it's easy to think of revolution as some big thing that happens. The result of some group of people organizing and planning and hitting the streets to protest either peacefully or violently. And I'm certainly aware that these things are necessary for the liberation of a people. In fact, I'm often confused by why, after four hundred years of killing, enslaving, and/or marginalizing Black, Brown, and Indigenous people, America believes itself immune to revolution. Especially since its founding is based on one. But that is the contradiction that is this country. The way it conveniently forgets its own actions, its own sins, while touting its exceptionalism.

So I get the big revolutions. But I also want us to consider the quiet revolts. The tiny protests we make every day. The decisions that Black folks make on a daily basis to no longer allow ourselves to be diminished or degraded. To silently decide to pull our children out of schools that don't serve them. To decide to intentionally move into communities with people who look like us, or to not move from communities that don't. Every time we decide that our worth, our joy, our lives, matter more than anything else, we are stomping down a system that refuses to let us heal and be. Every time we decide to be completely and authentically who we are as Black people, whatever that might look like, we are standing in opposition to those who try to make us believe that our only value is found in our proximity to Whiteness.

This reminds me of the distinct moment I decided that I didn't want to code-switch anymore. I had begun my career as an adult working in corporate America because I thought that was just what you did when you graduated from college—you got yourself a good job with benefits. I never thought I could pursue anything in the arts for real. I certainly never thought I could actually write for a living. Of course, I knew there were people who did it, but it was just not on my radar. So I went into corporate America, and of course there are rules. There's a culture. And in the late nineties, part of that culture required a tamping down of any overt Blackness in order to move up some arbitrary ladder that was really a booby-trapped obstacle course that most people failed. I couldn't be the fullness of who I am in terms of the way I spoke, wore my hair, or moved. All of those things needed to align with White standards of beauty and communication.

So I spent maybe five years in corporate before I just said, "Nah, this ain't me." I moved on to a field I thought would allow me more freedom. But interestingly enough, when I transitioned into academia after going to grad school and ultimately getting a job as a college professor, I realized that it wasn't that much different. Sure, there was a little bit more flexibility, but there was still a narrowly defined way I thought I needed to comport myself in the classroom. I was told to present myself in ways reminiscent of my experience in corporate. This despite White professors being allowed to show up to class in jeans or, gasp, flip-flops.

Nope. Not doing it.

By 2014, I'd published a few things and so I decided to take a break from teaching and make a detour into publishing. I ended up working as a managing editor at a religious publisher, and from the day I walked in for my interview I'd determined that I was no longer interested in being anything other than my glorious Black self.

But, if I'm honest, it was still hard to shake the whispers of respectability that were seeded deep in my bones. So while I spoke the way I wanted to speak and freely shared aspects of my culture with those who, in hindsight, probably didn't care much about it, I didn't do the things I loved to do with my hair. A seemingly insignificant issue for those who can't comprehend the things Black women have endured because of the way our hair grows out of our heads. Those who know me now know that one day you might see me with pink hair and the next day I might have long, waist-length braids. I take seriously the Black girl prerogative to change my texture, cut, color, or length. But I didn't do that much in *that* space.

Still, I did walk into that interview with an attitude I never had before. One that said, *I'm bringing value to you. If you want me, you're going to have to accept all that comes with me.* And I got the job. It was the first step. The first time I realized that maybe I didn't have to contort myself so much in order to get the things I wanted.

But this was a religious publisher, so I couldn't escape the impending reckoning. During this same time, I had begun my own process of unpacking my faith and considering the ways in which Christianity, particularly the White, Westernized versions of it, had been used to perpetuate White supremacy. Needless to say, working for a predominately White, conservative, evangelical publisher that was an arm of a missionary organization caused many tiny revolts as I tried to push and prod people toward inclusion who had no intention of ever *seeing* me beyond the labor I provided.

I ultimately came to the conclusion that I was done. If they couldn't handle my hair, my body, my clothes, my voice, my tone, or the way any of those things might transform over time, as humans are wont to do, then they couldn't have my gifts or my labor. I left that publisher and returned to academia with this firmly as my mantra.

I'll never forget being an adjunct professor at a community college and getting the wonderful, if not ironic, opportunity to do a professional development for other faculty on cultural competency and diversity. I was standing up there doing my thing and I could tell that everyone in the class was so engaged. It was a really wonderful experience. Afterward, a woman came up to me, apparently a full-time faculty member, and said, "I want to help you possibly get a full-time position here. I would love to just connect with you. I think you are such a wonderful teacher." And of course, my instinct was to downplay the compliment, but I didn't. I did good that time. I simply said, "Thank you so much." She asked for my LinkedIn profile and I sent it to her.

A couple of weeks later, I got a message from her saying: "I got a chance to look at your LinkedIn profile. It looks really good. I think where you're going to run into problems though is your look. It is too wild."

Record scratch.

I was so confused. At that time, I had pretty lengthy locks. But in an effort to somewhat appease the cultural standards, they were very neatly twisted and usually pulled into some conservative bun. I didn't know what she meant by "wild," but I could only guess that she meant "not straight." But I was different by then. My code-switching button was broken; whether we were talking about the way I spoke or fashion or beauty, I had no intention of fixing it. I deftly move in and out, back and forth from the King's English to African-American vernacular by choice. As an act of protest or sometimes just because, as Tabitha Brown might say, it's my business, I wore my hair the way I wanted (straight, curly, weaved, or wig). My level of unbotheredness was on a thousand by the time this woman got to me.

I just let it ride. And I kept showing up as my beautiful, brilliant, Black self. And interestingly enough, I ended up getting that full-time teaching position without her help. It was gratifying to stand in that first faculty meeting and be introduced as one of the new full-time faculty at the college and to have that same woman turn around and look at me.

With cherry red extensions in my hair.

I got the position being exactly who I was, regardless of what she or anyone else like her may have thought about it. I'm clear that my tiny revolution—me wearing my hair in the Blackest hairstyles possible—doesn't change policies in D.C. It might not have a global political impact. But these individual protests will pave the way for the Black girl coming behind me who sees me being my whole, Black self and realizes that she doesn't have to abandon herself in order to be successful. That who she is matters and is valuable. There's so much joy in being liberated in this way.

I know that it's hard to be Black still in some workplaces and environments. And people need to eat. But I'm also a firm believer that if you lose a job for some reason other than you aren't equipped or capable to do it, then it's actually the job that lost you.

Revolutions are happening every day. There are a bunch of them happening all around us.

Poet E. Ethelbert Miller wrote that "if we are to be activists of any kind, we should be motivated by what begins in the center of our hearts." Likewise, if true large-scale revolution is ever going to take place—if there ever will come a time when there is a complete overturning of the White supremacist systems that are at the root of our justice and social systems—it will likely come about because enough of our hearts have been lit with the fire of protest in our personal lives.

One thing is clear: these tiny revolts are small but rarely subtle. They are loud even when you can't hear them. Whether you are removing your child from a school that can't see them or wearing your blue hair to a job that you rock out at daily, these small actions are convicting for those who seek to oppress you. They are heard loud and clear at the level of soul and spirit. And all those who want to tell Black people to not play a card they actually dealt to us will have to get used to the noise.

13

The Fourth

Sometimes it was just about the meat. About all the preparations that happened the night before. The way Maw-Maw or Big Ma or Uncle So-and-So would season everything. Sometimes with basic salt, pepper, and garlic powder. Other times with a more complicated secret blend if they wanted to show out and get a little fancy. Big booties of pork, slabs of ribs, whole and pieces of chicken, vats of brine, all lined the stove and counters readied for the next day's festivities. Even though things wouldn't start popping until later the next afternoon, it was important to get things ready. To prepare. To make sure there was enough gallons of off-brand iced tea or Hi-C or Hawaiian Punch or, if things were tight and the crowd small, a couple of Tupperware pitchers of Kool-Aid made with extra, extra, *extra* sugar.

That was mostly grown-up stuff, though. All that preparing of the food, getting out the brown metal folding chairs that maybe, possibly, but who's going to tell, were stolen from the church. Lining up the six-foot-long tables that would stretch across Grandma's tiny backyard or the Auntie who thought she was better than everybody because she moved to the suburbs' big backyard or the picnic shelter at the public park. (In Louisville, it could be Shawnee, Chickasaw, Seneca, or Cherokee park depending on where you lived.) Yes, the grown-ups were responsible for those things. As kids, we just couldn't wait for the fun or the attention or the affection. We looked forward to the way our aunties would laugh and cackle about something in the back kitchen. The way the uncles would smoke and drink and talk loud about whether the Cardinals would win the NCAA championship or who caught the biggest fish or whether or not that was Buster they saw downtown or who got laid off or who was on that stuff.

For me, when it came to the food, I was mostly all about the mac and cheese and the hamburgers. I liked my burgers well done, just like my mama did. We weren't trying to see a lick of pink, and if we did we would ask for it to be put back on the grill for "about five or six more" minutes. I suppose some people would probably call it burnt nowadays, but that was just the way it was supposed to be. By early evening, the Spades or bid whist or domino or Pokeno games had begun. For the latter, folks would have their ziplock Baggies full of change at the ready. I remember one year, my mom saying, "Girl, I'm making your lunch money back off your aunties." That was back when lunch was 50 cents and an extra 10 cents could get you an extra chocolate milk.

But the most important part of the day for us kids was when the dark fully settled in the sky, turning the hot, humid days into hotter nights. We would push out the front door and onto the street—sticky because we ran through the sprinkler with our clothes on in ninety-degree heat and now the water and sweat clung to us. With the moon high and our worries low, we were itching for the lights and sounds that came from an uncle or three finally firing up the firecrackers. As the pow, pow, pow of smoky sparks streamed across the asphalt, excitement sizzled. The anticipation building for the finale event felt like too much to bear. I couldn't wait to hold the fire. At least that's what I used to call it.

"You be careful now, ya hear? Ain't nobody going to the hospital tonight."

Really, they were just sparklers. Colorful, flaming sticks our parents or friends or other family members would light for us. I'd twirl and spin as the sparks flew, the hypnotic flares drawing me into the joy of the moment. There was something about that light that attracted me. Their glow made me feel powerful even at six or seven or ten years old. I was transformed into a superhero like my favorite, Wonder Woman, and the idea that I could save anyone, but mostly myself, was intoxicating.

I didn't know too much about the history of my people in this country and all the complicated issues around Independence Day. I'm not sure whether that was a function of a school system that only had room for Martin Luther King, Jr. when it came to teaching African-American history or the typical obliviousness that comes with being a little kid. I just knew there was one day that, when night came, I could hold the fire. And when I asked other Black folks in my community about their traditions on the Fourth of July, there was that same common thread. Food and community and barbecues were the centerpieces of their experience. But also—a distinct awareness of a cultural partition. There always seemed to be two celebrations going on at once on the Fourth. The White folks did their thing with their patriotic music, flags, and parades. And we did ours—happy just for another day off or happy to see Nanny or Ma or Grandma smiling from ear to ear as everyone throws down on her fried chicken and collard greens or happy to show off the new dances to our cousins or to our elders in makeshift talent shows. I'm struck with a profound yearning as I remember how we'd hype up the worst dancer among us, laughing both with and at them, but always and forever in love.

In later years, we'd test the waters. Dipping our toes in the river of mixed company beyond just the occasional White girlfriend of a second cousin. This usually just meant heading downtown to see the fireworks. Even then, we were superconscious of the world around us. We understood that just as the fireworks were bigger, there was also something else bigger, if unspoken, about this country and its allegiances.

And now we know more. Our church chairs might have dried ketchup from all the Juneteenth celebrations from fifteen days before. Now, triggered by the sound of fireworks, I might sit in the backyard and meditate; accessing my sparks, holding my fire, from the inside. Just Jesus and me sitting by the big tree in full lotus, taking deep breaths and pondering our next move toward the liberation of my people. It's different, yes, but the same. The Fourth still gets to be what I or we or you say it is, if anything at all.

If not for celebration, always for community.

If not for family, then always for kinship.

But clearly, never ever for independence.

. . . as *resilience*

WE TESTIFY WITH EACH
NEW BREATH

MAY JOY FREE YOU TO

- *Invest in your soul care*
- *Hold tight to your humanity*
- *Harness the wind when storms come*
- *Set your babies free*
- *Liberate your laughter*
- *Leave, stay, and return*
- *Release any need for external acceptance*

14

What Gets Burned Off

Standing there watching the milk boil was a kind of meditation. My heart was heavy and my mind was crowded with what was mostly grief. I needed to recenter if I was going to even remotely see the day to its end. The liquid was still and white at first. Probably not expecting the simmer that was just around the corner. It looked like a cast-iron skillet-sized blanket of ice. Then the bubbles. It was a sign that just below the surface, things were heating up. I could see the resistance, though. The cold fighting the hot in a useless battle. Finally, there were bigger bubbles. Layers of white steam rising from the pan. Some of the milk was fully changed. The thick, creamy scent in the air was a sign that, in order to be of use to me and my cup of chai rooibos latte, parts of it had to change form and some parts would have to be burned off completely.

I've been thinking a lot about what gets lost in our freedom struggles as Black people. More succinctly, the cost incurred for change. There are plenty of books out there that highlight what we've gained as a result of the centuries of freedom movements our people have fought. I don't disagree with most of them. But it's equally important to consider what is lost in the steam, if you will. What gets burned off in order for our status and place in this world to change form?

Ashley McGirt, an activist and licensed mental health therapist, spoke with HuffPost on June 10, 2020, in an article titled "A Racial Trauma Therapist Breaks Down the Black Lives Matter Protests," about some of what is lost in the struggle of freedom. In particular, the impact of racial trauma on our bodies and minds:

> *The protests are deeper. There's a lot of built-up inner rage. There's a lot of truth coming out that has never really been to the forefront. . . .*
>
> *[These protests are] causing a lot of stress, a lot of exhaustion, anxiety. . . .*
>
> *Yet sometimes as a people, we're very resilient. We have a high level of emotional resilience, but our bodies don't and our bodies begin to break down.*
>
> *I've been seeing lots of people having nosebleeds because the pressure literally becomes compacted to where their nose starts to bleed. Their necks are hurting because we're walking around and bracing ourselves, like, "What's next?" . . .*
>
> *Racial trauma relates to the race-based stress that people of color, indigenous people and Black people experience from seeing other people of color, indigenous people being harmed publicly facing constant re-exposure to it.*
>
> *It's like post-traumatic stress disorder, but PTSD tends to*

sometimes be a singular incident. . . . With racial trauma, it's always ongoing, and it has a huge impact. It causes fear, hyper-vigilance, shame, guilt, anxiety, depression.

To be clear, it's racism that's causing these responses and not the protests. Without the constant, pervasive encounters with systemic racism, protests and revolts would never be needed. That said, the fight to claim or retain what is inherently ours is exhausting and does create dis-ease in the body. So the fire of racism turns up the heat on our protests and struggle, Whiteness and White supremacy resists the advancement of society, and while the change is inevitable, something gets lost in the ether. Specifically, some of our physical, mental, and emotional health is sacrificed.

We know this will happen. We accept this as our cost. But how do we mitigate it from being such an overwhelming toll? How do we keep from becoming too broken and tired and ill to enjoy the change, the freedom, whenever it arrives?

Dr. Joi Lewis, in her talk "Radical Trauma Healing and Liberation," poses a similar question: "How do we both cultivate joy and hold heartbreak at the same time. . . . Even in the midst of all these things, how do we know we are a people who have amazing and joyous things to embrace, how can we find joy even in the midst? We have this healing power that is in our own hands . . . [but] we don't get touched in loving kind ways enough."

Joy, particularly in the form of self-preservation, is the key to limiting the burn-off. I wonder what would happen if the majority of us chose the both/and approach to the fight for equal rights. We can march in the streets *and* make sure we are drinking water and eating healthily. We can run for office to try to undo policies that hurt our people or, as activists, make our demands known on the public stage, *and still* schedule time for therapy and soul care. We can rage *and* rest. We can resist *and* refresh. We can keep up with current events *and* shut off social media for a few hours. We can fight for justice for all Black folks *and* hold ourselves accountable to the ways internalized racism and misogynoir shows up in our own communities. We can raise our hands to the powers that be to challenge and appeal but *also* reach our hands out to one another in loving-kindness. The both/ and approach is hard, for sure. But hard has never been a question for Black folks. There are people out here who are and have been doing this work.

I was staring at that pan of boiling oat milk because there was an adjustment underway in my own life. I was considering a major shift—doubling down on my own healing work and helping others do the same—that would change the trajectory of my career and the dynamic of my relationships. The heat I felt simmering just below the surface was building and I was fighting it with everything I had. Despite knowing that the change was both necessary and inevitable. In hindsight, I don't think it was the change I was fighting as much as it was the comfort and stability that would be burned off that I was trying to salvage. And yet I didn't have any control over what was lost. I only had control over how I would transform that loss into something else, something even more vital in the moment.

We can't help that with every freedom fight we lose an incremental bit of our hope in a humanity that will one day treat Black and Indigenous people with empathy and respect. I see it happening with every new hashtag. George Floyd's murder ignited a global conversation on police brutality and racism, in general. Breonna Taylor's senseless murder created a visceral intersectional response that charged the movement even more. But the desensitization that comes with continuously watching Black men and women killed on-camera is a loss. The collective grief, and the trauma that comes out of that, is a loss. Our struggle to still hold on to joy in the midst of evidence that in four hundred years of living on these shores and a myriad of accomplishments and innovations, we are still at the mercy of Whiteness and its need for dominance and power is absolutely a loss.

Maybe there's a compromise. A resolution that requires less struggle and more quietude. I like the idea of engaging in refreshment as freedom. It undergirds the truth that freedom is inherent to us, a human right, and that we don't fight for it; we simply own it. And if it's stolen, we take it back. Because it's ours. What that looks like might vary. During the Summer of 2020 Black Lives Matter protests, the media tended to show only the righteously angry faces of protestors. The fists in the air and the chanting. But I actually loved seeing the videos of people singing and dancing and holding each other's hands in the streets. There was one couple in Philadelphia who even chose to get married during the protests. The dancing, laughter, and joy on their faces didn't diminish the seriousness of the cause we were all fighting for. They, in fact, had the right idea. Pardon me while I borrow from the Gen Z lexicon:

They big mad.
They hate to see it.

Our joy makes racist White folks mad. Our joy in the face of change fueled by their violence makes them even madder.

I'd never suggest diminishing the ways in which my ancestors and grandparents have fought for civil rights. There's so much we can learn from them, from their stories, for our present fights. But I also see the music and laughter and dancing, the burning of respectability politics to the ground, as a way to enact change while limiting the burn-off of our joy. In this way, our steam, our joy, though a very different form from our chants and our policy making, is weaponized on our behalf.

The fight for freedom has cost us some things, and the awareness of this is the first step to getting them back. Not in the form they were before. I can never turn steam back into milk. But maybe something wholly useful and equally as indispensable.

15

Inside Out

I can't be bothered to properly raise the two sets of mini-blinds hanging from the windows in my office. I suppose from the outside, it looks better when they're even with each other. They will, however, remain crooked because that just seems right. It's where my head is right now. Let the folks outside my home assume whatever they like about my preference for nonsymmetrical jalousie. It's been that kind of year.

A 1969 *Playbill* is sitting perilously close to the edge of my desk. It is one of my most prized possessions. Lorraine Hansberry stares out from its cover in all her young, gifted, and Black excellence. She had been dead for four years already, but just as this posthumous production implies, I imagine she is still very much alive. Very much wandering the perimeter of my imagination planting seeds of inspiration whenever she has the notion. This helps me.

There are also bottles everywhere. A bottle of water. A bottle of ginger mango juice. And bottles upon bottles of essential oils. A whiff of frankincense might beat back the twin demons of panic and anxiety just as well as lavender or ylang-ylang, but it's best to not be caught slipping. These bottles cradle the place where my work must begin. The space isn't clean, but I don't consider it messy either. It's just mine. The teakettle, the books of various shapes and genres. The heating pad draped across my lap because the aching in my muscles won't stop and doesn't care how much work I have to do. I decide to write this piece longhand, but the problem with that is that my mind moves light-years ahead of my hands and I can't get the words down fast enough. So what is perfect and well crafted in my brain is only sparse segments of chicken scratch. Then, an interruption. A verdict has been reached.

"Life in jail without parole."

I thought I knew, but apparently I didn't. You don't know how much Black life doesn't matter until you realize the lengths our system will go to in order to save the life of a man who murdered Black people. I'm clear that had Gregory Alan Bush been a Black man who killed two White people and endangered the lives of a myriad of others, not even his mental state would have kept him from seeing the electric chair.

People keep asking if me and my family are happy with the outcome. I'm not sure "happy" is the word I'd use. It has been two years since this philistine, Bush, walked into a Kroger grocery and decided that two people should die because they were Black. One of those individuals was my elder cousin Vickie. A woman who would have held Mr. Bush's hand and prayed with him if he needed it. The loss our family feels and the residue of the trauma that has yet to be seen is immense, so, of course, there's a part of me that wants this guy to fry. Everything in me wants him to feel his last moments seeping out of his body just like my cousin must have felt on that fateful day as he stood over her in the parking lot.

But there is another part of me that just wants him to rot. Wants him to live with those demons and have his spirit devoured from the inside out. That's the part of me this verdict satisfies. And yet it also feels so incredibly inadequate as a solution.

I've always been anti–death penalty. Especially in light of how it has been enacted here in the United States. And for the last few years, I've been studying the abolition of prisons. Before today, I've never wavered in my stance. In the beginning, it was my bright-eyed idealism that drove me. When I was sixteen and debating with whoever would listen, I argued that every life, no matter how wretched, deserves a chance at redemption even until the bitter end. But as life slapped me around a bit, my reasoning changed even if my position did not.

Admittedly, I went through a deeply religious season when I held on to the notion that the Grace gospel of Jesus negated the Old Testament mandate of an eye for an eye. The deconstruction of that same faith over the last decade meant that this sentiment burned out quick and fast. My current position isn't, in fact, rooted in any biblical position, nor is it based on any youthful sanguinity. It's firmly the result of knowing that, yes, every life matters and that must include the Black lives stolen by White men who are never forced to face conviction, much less the possibility of a death penalty. The vast disparities in our justice system mean that the death penalty needs to be abolished completely. Some argue that if the state can kill a Black man for being an accomplice to a murder (see: Brandon Bernard) then they must also kill the White man who kills with intention and in cold blood.

My traumatized heart wants this to be true and right.

But just like my blinds, the perception of what's right or equal depends on where one is sitting. On the inside or the out. I know the blood of my cousin would never cry out for vengeance. It wasn't in her makeup. But I also get that because of the way White folks have violated and pillaged Black and Brown bodies, it feels like justice should be meted out in an equally violent way.

Deep down below my pain, my soul resonates with the exact opposite. It says that because Brandon should have never died, Gregory Bush shouldn't either. It says the criminal justice system itself needs a complete overhaul, and a moratorium on the most barbaric aspects of that system must apply to everyone. Including the ones most deserving in my mind.

In my body, this feels like a betrayal. My insides stay twisted into knots knowing this man is breathing, but our Vickie is not. Yes, I can stand on higher ground and pronounce the system so broken that no one should die at its hands, but what do I do when, simultaneously, I desire for at least one man to absolutely die at its hands? A system imbued with the same White supremacist ideals that empowered him to kill my cousin in the first place? This is the tension in which I live. This is the asymmetry of my existence.

I suspect there are many Black folks who live in this space with me. We rightfully desire justice for the violence inflicted on us. We rightfully demand that the ones who kill us be held to account. But we also wrestle with a powerful and necessary resistance to becoming like our oppressors. We try our damndest to resist acting out in even seemingly justified violence against White folks because we have maintained our humanity in ways that many of them have long lost.

In the same ways that we have to reckon with the transgenerational trauma of our history in the West, White people must also reckon with the trauma of complicity when it comes to the brutality that exists in their own bloodlines. The ability to enslave a whole group of people, to enjoy meals and laugh with their children as other humans are lynched from trees, undeniably created a multi-generational hardening of their own capacity for empathy and benevolence. This translates into being able to watch video after video of Black people being blatantly and obviously brutalized and still comfortably go about one's merry day. Meanwhile, Black folks continue to grip—though with less and less earnestness—our ace in the hole that wins every game, every time: our humanity.

> *Negroes*
> *Sweet and docile,*
> *Meek, humble, and kind:*
> *Beware the day*
> *They change their minds!*
>
> *Wind*
> *In the cotton fields,*
> *Gentle breeze:*
> *Beware the hour*
> *It uproots trees!*
> —Langston Hughes

So far, we've chosen to laugh in the faces of our murderers. Because some of us believe that it's the laughter that keeps us whole. We've chosen to keep bouncing back. To keep being resilient as evidence of their failure at true annihilation. In this way, even their savagery is cheapened into mediocrity. Even when they kill us, they can't kill us.

And yes, I understand why people were angry when family members of a recent victim of police brutality announced their forgiveness of the murderer. Even I was appalled, primarily by how their choice was held up as a standard for the way the collective "should" respond. I certainly believe in forgiveness as praxis. Even our favorite gurus/teachers/pastors/psychotherapists recommend forgiveness as a way to heal from the traumatic events of our lives. But the challenge with forgiveness in the context of these racially motivated killings is the lack of accountability we see. That asymmetry doesn't allow for those of us who are affected to extrapolate the past from the present, to engage with the concept that "time heals all wounds," in order to begin healing. Every new hashtag is a new injury and a new reminder of old pains. The lack of justice creates a situation where the act of forgiveness becomes nothing but performance art as opposed to one of many steps back to wholeness.

Still, there is a part of me that understands there needs to be another route; another type of response other than violence. To be clear: this is no argument for respectability. I'm not one who was terribly upset at alleged rioters during the otherwise peaceful protests that happened across the country in the Summer of 2020. This is mostly because I've read books. I know that change often comes with revolution. And revolution often comes with its share of fire and bloodshed. I also know that there are ten or more generations' worth of pain walking those streets. Someone resolving to take what they can is not in the least worrisome when you understand that they are acting out of the exhausting realization that way too much of what actually matters was stolen from them.

But I do wonder if our resilience as a people is connected to our continuous hold on our own humanity. Whether in doing so, we shine a piercing light on the barbaric nature of some White folks who are, in fact, the descendants of colonizers and/or slavers. And if we decide upon a shift in our approach, do we even want that kind of power? Do we want to relinquish our capacity to love, to be human, in exchange for some perceived dominance? I'm not sure I do. I want to hold on to what makes me spiritually and emotionally sound. What made my Vickie better than Bush by a long shot.

So I suppose from the outside, just like my mini-blinds, the disparities are clear. Without any doubt, they should be righted. But I also know that things are way more complicated where I sit. Where many Black folks sit. On this side, those same disparities reveal the sustaining "in spite of" power of Black resilience. And that is fine. For now.

16

Laugh Loudly and Often: A Historical Conversation

I never thought I'd say it. Never thought I'd get to this place. But I have finally grown tired of the big city.

Whaaat?

Yes, it's true.

In my early twenties, when life seemed spread out in front of me like a smorgasbord of possibilities, I could not wait to leave Kentucky. And in true coming-of-age Lifetime movie fashion, off I went to Chicago and then later to the New York area and Philadelphia. But in the last couple of years, I have been wanting, not just more space physically, not just more literal space, but also more emotional and spiritual space. For a long time, being in a large metropolitan area served me well. I'm absolutely grateful for the lessons I learned there. But right now, I feel like my soul is crowded. There's no room for me to stretch out and just be. What's good for one season is not necessarily what's best for the next, and in this one I'm longing for land and space.

It's been nearly twenty-five years since I set out for Chicago, and when I think about how I want to live the rest of my years on this earth I dream about being able to step out into a garden or being able to walk the expanse of a property that bears my name and the name of my child. I think about how grounding the grass feels on my bare feet and how the birds chitchat with one another every morning in places where they aren't constantly interrupted by planes, trains, and automobiles, or the rapping teenager in Beats headphones who seemingly thinks he can keep up with Kendrick's flow.

So recently my husband and I decided that we would put our dream in motion. We are going to buy some land. Not exactly ready to move back south, we decided to look for a home with acreage in the Jersey or Delaware shore areas because as much as I love land, I love water more. The ocean is a salve for my spirit and I've spent hours taking in its beauty. We also needed to still be close to our work, friends, and other obligations in Philly, so South Jersey and Delaware felt like the best options.

I also made a decision several years ago that I never wanted to live or work in an all-White anything. Mostly for my own sense of emotional and physical safety. I refuse to subject my daughter to the hostility, overt or subtle, that inevitably comes with being the *only* one. The only Black person in her class. The only Black kid in her neighborhood.

My desire for a multi-cultural or diverse neighborhood presented us with a slight problem, though. I was asking for a home with land. In a semi-rural area. Near the beach. That also had plenty of Black folks who lived there.

Umm, sure. Please direct me to this utopia, stat!

In researching some of the towns in the area, I came across some information that blew my mind. It's really weird how it happened. I was investigating Galloway Township because I'd read quite a bit about McKee City in nearby Hamilton Township—a town founded by Colonel John McKee, the wealthiest Black man in America at his death in 1902. After reading everything about the history of that town, I started looking up information about neighboring Galloway, and came across the name of Abraham Galloway. What? Was this another Black man who founded a town in southern New Jersey?

Well, no.

Abraham Galloway literally has absolutely nothing to do with Galloway Township in New Jersey. The Googles had led me astray.

Or had they?

I've always been drawn to the untold story. The untaught history. I'm just as drawn to the story of Claudette Colvin as I am proud of Rosa Parks. I'm just as fascinated by Alice Allison Dunnigan as I am impressed by April Ryan. So when I found Mr. Galloway, I fell down the rabbit hole and traversed the dimensions to hear what this man had to say to me from across the cosmos. It's a kind of time traveling I like to do. Maybe not consciously but certainly with intention.

There is something to be said about knowing exactly who you are, exactly what you want, and, despite whatever limitations you face, going after it, Tracey.

In 1837, Galloway was born in Smithville, North Carolina, to an enslaved African woman and a White man. From childhood, he was trained as a brickmaker and often traveled between the plantation and Wilmington, North Carolina, a popular port for cotton.

I know that even the European blood running through these veins doesn't absolve me of my responsibility to serve and free my people. Though we speak across the expanse of time and space, this is by far still true for you.

Hearing through the grapevine that there was something called the Underground Railroad, he stowed away on one of the ships heading north, escaping the fumigation that was often done to catch those escaping slavery. Assisted by abolitionists in Philadelphia, he ultimately ended up in Ontario, Canada—out of the reach of fugitive slave laws.

People believe that when you escape a hardship, that when you liberate yourself, then your concerns are over. I can assure you they are not, my friend. In fact, I'm not sure anyone can ever be settled in heart and mind if their friends and family and even those they do not know are left in bondage. In whatever form that servitude may take. There's no rest in Canada when so many are still under the lash in North Carolina.

Returning to the South multiple times to assist in helping enslaved Africans escape to freedom, Galloway became a spy for the Union army during the Civil War. Even before enslaved men were allowed to fight in the war, Union officers relied on Black men and women who had escaped the South to help them navigate the terrain and make inroads into Confederate territory. Abraham Galloway was responsible for helping the Union establish those connections with other Black men and women, but he did not trust the Union at all. Especially after being abandoned by troops after a loss in battle. He'd also seen too many instances where Black soldiers were massacred with the Union turning a blind eye. But he was good at what he did. And so when the Union came knocking once more—this time for his assistance with Negro troops—he negotiated with them. Equal pay, protection for the Negro troops' families, and the designation of the enslaved as prisoners of war—and not property—were the items at the top of his list. In today's vernacular, Galloway played zero games.

Let them believe they are using you, Tracey. It's often the only way to fly under the radar. Before they even realize what has happened, when they finally come up for air after fighting their wars and making their declarations, you will have accomplished your goals and simultaneously thwarted their plans for you.

After the war, Galloway didn't stop his pursuit of full liberation and equality. He understood that there were now thousands of newly freed Black men and women and children who needed assistance. So he became a leader in multiple organizations, including a delegation of Black leaders who spoke with President Abraham Lincoln. He also was one of many Black men who ran for office during Reconstruction. He was a delegate to the North Carolina Convention of 1868 and ultimately became the state's first Black presidential elector and one of the first Black senators during this era.

I say over and over that liberty is worth dying for. And it is. But you are less likely to die for your freedom if you have a strategy.

At every turn, Galloway proved that to outmaneuver White supremacy, one had to fearlessly step into its sphere and challenge its very existence. His accomplishments were unparalleled, despite his being unable to read or write. But one of the most fascinating parts of our conversation came with the realization that his true power lay in his sly grin and the joy he kept hot and heavy in his hands.

Aha! Exactly. Humor is not only evidence of your humanity; it's a devastating blow to the consciousness of a White man who refuses to see you. I've heard that I am perceived to be a bit gregarious in nature, and I suppose this is true. Others have said I laugh loudly and often. This too is true. I've found that my joy is the most irritating to those who are righteously indignant at my audacity to walk around like I'm free.

The systems of the supernatural, what my ancestors might call the unseen, are rarely ever ordered. So I'm grateful for the ways in which Galloway pierced the sky and made his presence known to me in this engagement. Between his enslavement and his suffrage, he embodied resilience in a way I needed to see. In a way I needed to understand was accessible to me. His story gives me permission to stand nose to nose with the racism, sexism, and misogynoir that regularly tries to snare me, smirk with the knowledge of the breadth of ancestral virtues I hold inside, and with audaciousness walk through this life like I'm truly free.

17

I Don't Have to Know

The certainty you're craving makes you suffer more
than the uncertainty you're avoiding.

—Maxime Lagacé

I watch the purple clouds move across the backdrop of a hot
pink sky. This is the holy performance I receive some mornings as I stare at the sun emerging from the Philadelphia skyline
from my bedroom window. I'd like to think that the Master
Artist paints this canvas just for me each morning as a reminder
that this same galactic capacity for creation lies within these
creaking arms and legs, this forgetful and oft-burdened brain,
this severely cracked but not quite broken heart. Even when the
bright colors settle on their vibrant but expected blue, I try to
contain it all. Knowing full well, I can't.

The morning sunrise in all its various iterations reminds me
that I know enough and nothing at all. I'm supposed to be okay
with that. But there are at least a million things I still do not
know, and if I'm honest, that makes me want to spit fire. Since I
was a child, I found refuge in knowing. It was a safe place. Being

the resident know-it-all in class meant, in my mind, that I had value. And since I struggled to grasp my own value in any other space, I followed the yellow brick road of knowledge acquisition to my own personal Oz.

It's why in the past I read books and told stories. And maybe even why I still do. It's why I made up answers if I legitimately didn't have one. And, yes, maybe why I still do. I wrapped myself in a cloak of sure outcomes and refused to accept that there was and is a place and time when *not* knowing is not only real but also necessary.

The irony in all of this is that I embraced faith and religion fairly quickly. I was introduced to Jesus at nine years old at my aunt's small, storefront Pentecostal church in Vine Grove, Kentucky. And by all accounts, the start of my faith journey should have been the ultimate demonstration of my consent to abandon certainty. One of the core tenets being that "faith is the . . . evidence of things not seen."

But unfortunately, the version of Jesus I was taught to embrace was one rooted in very clear binaries. It proffered that the Word is true and anything that is not explicitly found in said Word is not. It was almost as if this new faith of mine amplified my need for certainty. Religion heightened what was a very real trauma response for me, and for many Black folks.

Black people have always had a reason to embrace certainty. The dogmatism we found in religion was appealing because of the dubious ways in which our daily lives would play out—the anticipation of violence; of discrimination. A survival mechanism was necessary. There was a need to embrace something that gave us firm lines and boundaries; rules to follow. It meant that if we could create clear demarcations for how to move through the world, then we could somehow make sense of the nonsensical things that happened to us.

This is the birthplace of what we now call respectability politics. We make the mistake of believing that if we have a certain amount of money or if we look a certain way or if we don't dress a particular way or if we wear our hair a certain way that somehow we'll be shielded from White supremacy in all of its schemes and iterations. The truth is, we won't be. The truth is that respectability and even the lines that are drawn by religion have never protected us from the violations of racist White folks.

But how do we live with that knowledge? How can we live day to day knowing that there is literally nothing we can do about the way we are seen and treated in this world? Particularly when we think about our mothers and fathers, our grandmothers and grandfathers post-Reconstruction and in the early twentieth century. If we have nothing to grab on, hold to, no certainties to hold, then how do we live?

So as much as many of us Black folks who identify as people of faith would like to believe that we grabbed on to religion solely for some God-ordained reason (a truth I won't debate), another significant reality is that holding on to the certainty of religion, particularly this sense of boundaries and respectable lines, gives us a semblance of safety, even if it isn't real. I think that's why Black church folks like the language of favor. We say things like "God favored him" or "the favor of the Lord is with her." Because, of course, if we see ourselves as favored in any way, then maybe we can escape what clearly seems like a lack of favor in the larger world.

Interestingly enough, I hold in my heart all the grace in the world for these same church folks and beliefs. Because I know how that kind of singular certainty has kept so many of us alive for a lot longer than the outside world might have intended. I just wish we hadn't gotten to the point where we turned it all on ourselves. The church was a grounding force in the civil rights movement of the fifties and sixties because it invested in the advancement of Black folks as a collective. It also provided a safe haven—patriarchy notwithstanding—for those who needed community, belonging, and love (no matter how tough). But when progress and prosperity (mostly indicated by proximity to Whiteness) seemed at least somewhat attainable, what was left exposed was all the ways in which the church had made respectability something akin to a tenet of the faith.

Go to any traditional Black church service and you're bound to hear someone in typical call-and-response fashion yell out, "Let him use ya!" to whoever is speaking or singing. It's an exhortation. An encouragement. And I'm clear that we so need both. We need people to say, "Keep going, baby." But/and we also need people to say, "Be still, baby. You are worthy just as you are, love." Unfortunately, a commitment to certainty doesn't abide this well. Cole Arthur Riley of Black Liturgies on Instagram posed two powerful questions during Lent 2021: What if God doesn't always want to use you? What if sometimes God simply wants to *be* with you?

For me, the investment in certainty was an intoxicating elixir. Some might even say a slippery slope. I liked the fact that there were Bible verses I could memorize that could lead to Sunday school Bible quizzes I could ace, which would ultimately lead to affirmations by Sister So-and-So and Brother Such-and-Such. Bingo! A direct link between my performance and my value that would chase me for another thirty years. My faith journey was riddled with padlocks and combination codes that allowed me to double down on my obsession with knowing all the things.

So what happens when the veil is removed? When the walls tumble and crumble under the weight of a life that rarely goes according to plan and people who cannot be controlled, and a faith that is unraveled by the undeniable realization that some of what folks taught me over the years was more about their own longings, convoluting the actual teachings of Jesus? For most of us, that's when the cracks in our souls are revealed.

They start as something tiny. Someone dropped my heart when I was seven or eight or nine and that singular puncture created a hairline fracture that has chased the ends of me since forever. Like a broken vase, the cracks threaten to shatter me completely some days, to the point where I've wondered how I was even holding myself together. But then I remember that unknowable, divine light that lives deep within. The light shining through those cracks was and is my miracle.

I recall lying on the couch in my one-bedroom apartment in a part of Philadelphia that people who grew up there called The Bottom. I was crying. It was apropos. I was in between career paths trying to decide whether I would stay in academia or continue pursuing my dreams of writing and publishing. I was in the beginning of a relationship that still was going through all of the uncertainties of new love. My heart was leaking my ambition, my desires for love and acceptance, and the hope that I would matter to someone somewhere someday. This time, there was no sobbing or wailing. It was just me, body curled into myself, face silently soaking in liquid sorrow, and the realization that I did not know anything. I had a lot of information, yes. I had read books. I'd followed the desires of my heart from Kentucky to Chicago to New Jersey to New York and then to Philly. I'd crafted me a life. But something was missing. True love? Maybe. Joy? For sure. Authenticity? Absolutely. I could probably name a million things. But there were no clear answers. No maps to any of these destinations. The pain came in shock waves, because I didn't know *how* to obtain any of it. I was being forced to reckon with the understanding that I'd never known.

I'd been performing for so long. Dancing every dance. Knowing every answer. And yet I was no more celebrated, no more loved, no more protected, than when I waved my hand wildly to answer the Bible quiz questions decades before.

Then came the whisper. It wasn't audible. It was a movement buried deep in my gut. My tears had quieted the noise in my mind. The light had pierced my cracks.

You are more well than you feel.

You are more well than you feel.

You are more well than you feel.

My first reaction, and what I would accept for many years afterward, was that "well" was referencing my physical health. I'd struggled with chronic pain and fatigue for so long that I thought maybe this was my spirit letting me know that my physical ailments were linked to something else; maybe physiological responses to trauma. To a certain extent, this was true. But it would take many more years for me to figure out that "well" was speaking to my own sense of self-worth. That I'd been centering the wrong people, places, and things as a baseline for my own value.

I was enough. Right then and there. With snot and dried tears streaking my cheeks. In my cheap apartment in Philly's Bottom sharing an internet Wi-Fi code with my downstairs neighbor. And right here and now. In my home watching purple clouds dance across a hot pink sky. There are things to be certain of, for sure. Largely that if we live another day then we have another day to live. That any love we might need can show up in the way we talk to and with one another. That the capacity to hold one another down when times get hard is a kind of superpower. Sharing flour and eggs on the off week of our pay period. Giving someone a ride to work. Sharing someone's post about their new business venture. But the suspension of certainty in matters of the heart and spirit is necessary if we are to heal.

It is okay that there are things I do not and cannot know. That fact does not have to make me want to spit fire or cause deep sadness. It just is. And even in that gray area, I can have an unspeakable joy arise from nowhere and require no investigation. I can sit in that joy and receive its power.

Even writing that feels strange. I want to go back and edit that last line. Take a word out. Add a qualifier. Try to paint a more reasonable picture of what joy looks like outside of the binaries given to us by churches and schools and a society so beholden to certainties. But I won't. I'll let it ride. And stay committed to the journey even if I never see or know the outcome.

18

Joy as Gap Filler

The White woman on the screen seemed like she was of the kind and harmless variety. The type who battled her inner Karen tendencies like Luke Skywalker in the Star Wars saga and usually, mostly, came out on top.

In a soft, gentle tone, she said, "If it's safe to do so, close your eyes and see yourself at the age of the rift. Take her in. What is she doing? Ask her what she needs. It's okay if she won't look at you. She might not be able to trust you yet."

The inner child meditation I'd been doing for several weeks required me to visualize myself interacting with my younger self. It was one of the hardest exercises I'd ever participated in. The first thing I noticed when I attempted to engage with elementary school Tracey was the gaps in my memories. At first, I could only see her hair—cornrows on some days, two large plaited ponytails on others. But I could never see her face. After overcoming that through the use of old pictures, I then struggled with seeing the room eight-year-old me was in or recognizing the voices that hovered over both of us. It was frustrating. I ached to remember it all, but the images would only appear in fragments. I knew my inner child was blurring my vision for a reason. Probably to keep me and her safe.

She had every right to do this.

Writers are expected to have really rich lives from which to draw our narratives. In fact, my favorite writers know how to interrogate their feelings about any given situation going on with them personally or in the larger world. There is a hyper self-awareness that I share with them, but while going through this particular type of healing journey I hadn't yet gotten to the point where I felt free enough to unleash a level of vulnerability that would allow me to be okay no matter what my memories revealed. There was a block there and the question I kept revisiting was: How does one be Black, a woman, have joy, and stay safe all at the same time?

My life taught me that I could only have one or two of those at any given time. I could embrace who I am fully as a Black woman and maybe I could experience occasions of joy because of that, but doing so might mean I would never feel safe. To relax my mind, heart, and body might mean opening myself up to harm. In fact, complete physical or mental relaxation has always felt like death to me. It's a parting gift of PTSD.

Now, if you'd asked me about this five years ago, I wouldn't have believed you. Or at least I would have pretended to not believe you. In recent years, though, the evidence had become increasingly clear. For at least a decade, if not more, I was walking around with every major muscle in my body clenched tight in a perpetual state of contraction. Doctor after doctor tried to give it a name, but at the end of the day, my body was simply responding to all the triggering information around me and had established that danger was imminent. It rang a cortisol gong that sounded the alarm on potential stress.

It knew that innocence wasn't mine for the keeping and naïveté wasn't useful if I wanted to live. I had to be ready to fight, fly, or freeze depending on the situation. Fight was usually my trauma response of choice.

It's scary to admit here on these pages that, at nearly forty-six years old, I am just learning how to relax for real. That I have a visceral physical reaction when I try to release my muscles or stop bracing for impact. Tears randomly fall. Muscles spontaneously start to quake. It's like my whole body becomes a living Black Twitter meme screaming, "Oh no, baby. What is you doing?" It's terribly frustrating, because I'm always aware of the ongoing debate in my mind between two parts of me. One who says, *If you let go, then you're not going to know when the next bad thing is going to happen. It's going to catch you off guard and you will be hurt.* The other part of me, the logical side, knows I'm doing more damage by living in a constant state of stress, but she has a tough row to hoe. The former voice has experience on her side. Sis has receipts that are CVS long. She has seen when the moments I felt the most free turned into moments when that freedom was stolen. The loss of my innocence as a child. The taking of my body as a young adult. The car that didn't stay in its own lane. The towers that fell. The relationships that went left. The backstabbers on the job who used to be friends. The Black men and women dying in the streets at the hands of police. The family members lost to the hands of mentally ill White folks who only see Brown skin as opposed to a beautiful heart.

It's hard to pinpoint the ways that relaxation serves me. I know that I should rest, but I also know that in my resting, the anticipation of the next thing happening feels too great. Too hard. I feel it in my chest, this sense that I won't survive the next thing. I must protect myself. Again, I ask, how does one be Black, a woman, have joy, and stay safe all at the same time?

At any moment, even the mundane and uneventful ones, the ones when you are minding your business or doing something you've always done, your life can be taken away. In an instant. Death rarely gives a warning. Even those with terminal illness don't have their transition marked on a calendar. Still, the sudden way my body can be wounded makes me tremble. Keeps me on edge. There is hardly ever a preamble or prologue. It steals my breath away every single time I dare to think about what it means to live in this skin.

The wall slide and piercing wail that escaped my body after receiving the horrific news that a White man had murdered my elder cousin could not compare to the way my body would respond over the following two years. The way the fear of racial violence took up residence in my being like an unwelcome squatter claiming ownership of this physical and spiritual home. I didn't enter a grocery for eight months afterward. The bright fluorescent lights made me dizzy. The wide aisles made me nervous. The lack of readily visible exits in the back of the building set off alarms in the back of my head. Even as I write this, I recall the feeling in my body. How the last remnants of safety and security that I'd piecemealed together from my past in order to breathe had quickly dissolved. There was no place I was safe. There's no place where any of us were safe.

I wonder if those who knew Eric Garner have this kind of trouble when they enter a corner store. Or if Trayvon's mom can stand to see a pack of Skittles. Or if Breonna Taylor's mother can ever really fall asleep. Or if my great-great-grandmother remembered the trees that bore the weight of Mr. So-and-So whenever she visited a park.

For me, there is one more gap in my soul because of that day. Darkness between the light. Parts of my life song where the record skips. My panic attacks are more like those few seconds in the subway when the train is barreling through the dark between stations. Anything can happen. And I can't stop it.

But it's in the recognition of those feelings of helplessness, in the presence of those fears, where we can draw the strength to line the pockets of our souls with hope. One of the things that White supremacy does well is exploit our fear. It riles up the need for sovereignty in White folks. It tamps down the dynamism of Black folks. It's the latter that steals our joy.

I used to think that the way to experience more joy in my life was to completely get rid of my fear. Unfortunately, I'd become friends with it. My fears were familiar to me. So the idea of eliminating them in order to experience a joy I was still not sure was mine to have felt like some kind of terrible surgical extraction. Because of this, I often chose the devil I know.

It took years for me to realize that I actually did not have to rid myself of all fear in order to know joy. I wasn't required to be oblivious to what was going on in the world in order to recognize or even enact moments of reprieve. Joy is perfectly capable of living alongside fear. Some would argue that it blooms there— ever reflective, ever the balm. In fact, when I lean into my fear, sit with it, become curious about it, and try to understand its source—where it comes from, who are its people—then it tends to dissipate on its own. Fear cannot hold itself together very long in the light of truth and love. And the very things we do sometimes to try to eliminate fear—not talking about it, not exposing it, not giving it air by sharing our stories, not being vulnerable— actually amplify it. When we hide from it, ignore it, we actually help the monster grow.

Denying my fears or trying to wrestle them into submission was only going to push me further into the darkness. Shining a light on them, embracing them, actually gives me the opportunity to find the gaps and to fill those gaps with moments of joy. To watch as that joy begins to eat away at the fear. Because once you recognize what joy feels like, know what it feels like to call it up when you need it, be present enough to know that *this* is a joyful moment, *this* is an instance you should be grateful for, then it diminishes the fear. It has no choice but to shrink in the face of joy.

After grieving my cousin's murder and then being smacked around by the COVID-19 pandemic, I genuinely feared stepping outside my door. But instead of choosing the darkness, I sat with that fear. I explored why I thought that the only truth was the one that ended in my death or the death of a family member. Sure, there were receipts that said it was possible that if I got pulled over by a cop, I could die. There were also receipts that said I might not. I learned to hold the tension of those two things in my mind and body, unpacking them, so I could step foot outside my door.

Black folks have a healthy fear of the White supremacist systems that threaten our lives almost daily in this country. But it doesn't have to be the only thing that we hold on to. That awareness can live alongside our wonders and delights. In truth, it always has. I'm not saying anything new, right? We have always lived this way. It's the reason why we've been so resilient. We allow our joy, our ability to see good in the midst of evil, to live in the company of our awareness of where we stand in the minds of some White folks in this country. Joy and hope has been the thread that has held the tapestry of our collective endurance together. If we lose hope, if we forgo our capacity for joy, I'm afraid we will lose a generation of people who have finally decided that hope doesn't work. And I get it. No judgment here. I'm clear that the standard I use to judge my people will be the standard used to judge me when my fears overwhelm me. So let my standard always be love. Let me simultaneously say, "Lean into your fear," while also understanding why after four-hundred-plus years that seems fruitless at best. Let me hold space for every person who finds themselves on the less affirming end of the joy/pain spectrum and let them know they are not alone. As prolific author Kiese Laymon once wrote, "We are all at least the second person to deal with what we're feeling." But just as we are never alone in our struggle, we are also never alone in our joy. Let's set about reclaiming it together.

19

Because They Are Watching

"**P**ut your shoes on, K!"

"Okay, Mommy!"

Even without looking, the sound of little brown feet pitter-pattering against the hardwood floor lets me know that she's headed to the mountain of shoes I can never stop from accumulating by the front door. Daddy's "mowing the lawn" sneakers, two or three pairs of Mommy's sandals, and two pairs of her own shoes are piled messily by the coatrack.

"I got 'em, Mommy!" she calls out with a giggle.

My mommy gut says something ain't right. You know the mommy gut, right? It's that sixth sense that tells you that your child is up to something even if you don't actually see them up to something.

When I walk into the living room from the kitchen, K is now caught up in full-blown laughter. Chuckles are spilling out of her from every which way.

She's put on shoes all right. Not her pink and orange sneakers. Not her white, blinged-out sandals. Nope. Baby Girl's tiny toes have found their way into *my* shoes. There she is scooting across the floor in these monstrous black leather wedges with the straps only barely flailing behind her.

"Mommy's shoes big!" she says between giggles.

"I wear Mommy shoes," she says as she walks like a mini-Frankenstein with her arms straight out to keep her balance.

She wants to walk in my shoes, huh?

I ponder this for a minute as I watch her; then I come to a conclusion that might have been way too deep for the moment.

If it's up to me, she will not ever walk in my shoes.

That bad, huh?

Well, it depends on your perspective.

No matter how much we want it to be true, Black joy isn't Black happiness. I can laugh heartily at my sweet girl, in that moment, and experience happiness at her silliness. But Black joy is the reason why I can see my child, my mirror, do something like try on my shoes, know that she will try to mimic me in more ways than that, and still want different and better for her. It is the destiny I can see for my daughter that I cannot imagine for myself. And I can't see it for myself because my life is very much linked to the personal and collective traumas I've experienced as a Black person. Experiences she's yet to have but, if our world continues on its current track, inevitably will.

As a child, I was molested. As a young adult, I was raped. In between those years, I wrestled with poor self-esteem and a desperate desire to please. I cared deeply what people thought about me but assumed that most people didn't think much. I encountered the condescension of racists who would not concede to the gifts of imagination I held. As a result, I used overachievement and ambition to cover up a broken heart and spirit. I overcompensated with my intellect and so, on paper, I looked pretty damn good. My soul was an entirely different story.

I saw glimpses of my true self in my thirties only to be slapped around by bad relationships, bouts of depression, a serious case of PTSD, and a couple of miscarriages. Add to that the constant pervasiveness of racism, racial microaggressions, patriarchy, and misogyny and through *that* lens it's been a rough ride to finding joy of any kind, much less anything specific to who I am as a Black woman.

My shoes are, as my southern family would say, run-over something terrible.

But here's another lens: I graduated early from college and followed up a bachelor's degree with two master's degrees. I wrote my first book at twenty-seven, signed my first book deal at thirty-four, and I've been able to piece together a career out of writing and teaching for the last decade. I've run businesses and helped others launch theirs. I married my friend at thirty-three and finally gave birth to the most beautiful little girl I've ever seen at thirty-six. At forty-five now, I have five years of therapy and deep trauma work under my belt as well as an ever-evolving spiritual practice to hold me down.

So from *that* angle, my shoes have held up pretty well, I suppose.

I've found power in my joy. Yes, that power is sourced in pain, but that pain has only provided a supercharge to my joy that I can now wield expertly against any injustice that comes my way. It's the strongest strategy I have at my disposal.

Yet as much joy as I've been able to piece together despite internal and external forces, I still maintain that I would never want my daughter to walk in my shoes.

And it's not necessarily because of the tragic stuff in my past either. Of course I don't want her to experience the awful, ugly, heart-wrenching pains I've lived through, but the reason why I don't want her to walk my path is much simpler than that.

Bottom line: my shoes don't fit. Just like when she puts her toddler feet in my grown-woman sandals, she cannot walk upright and confidently in my life's shoes. Yes, she is so much like me I often call her my mirror. Yes, by virtue of being my child, she will deal with the generational stuff that will inevitably come up as she wrestles with her own identity. Yes, as a Black woman living in America she will likely encounter racism and sexism in all the ways that I have and, at the rate this country is spiraling, maybe worse. But at the end of the day, my journey cannot be hers. Parents who try to re-create the lives they wanted through their children or who force their kids to take the routes they did are just wrong.

My daughter will have her own hardships and failures, for sure. Her own victories and triumphs, most definitely. But trust, when *she's* in her forties she will look back over her life and not see her mother's story but the story of her own life, born from a combination of her own choices and God's purpose. I hope it's mostly the latter. I pray even now that it will be. As her parents, her dad and I will set boundaries, guide her, talk to her, and support her while she is a child, but the choices she makes and the experiences she has later will be her own. Her experience of joy will be shaped by us, for sure. Like an archer pointing our bow and arrow in the direction of the ideal target, we will do our best in light of the systemic challenges to set the trajectory of her life in the direction of love, peace, joy, patience, discipline, grace, mercy, fun, and prosperity.

But we do not control the wind.

Boy, do I wish we did.

The winds of life (which include her own will) can change her destiny, I know. But I think it will still work out for her good. Even the things we see on television that scare the living daylights out of me as I consider sending her out into a world that will likely not see her the way we do. I've seen the wind turn in my life. I know how powerful it is. I also know how I've used that same wind, much like a surfer uses the waves, to bounce back in every area of my life. So as scary as it is to watch my nearly three-year-old try to walk in my shoes and realize that one day she will walk fully in her own, have her own great, good, bad, and ugly experiences, there's comfort in believing that there is something larger in control and, no matter what, she will be all right.

Hope is believing she will be all right.

20

Leaving Louisville: Part 2

TO GO, STAY, OR RETURN

Thirty days is all it took. Within thirty days of graduating undergrad, I was out. As a twenty-one-year-old Black girl from Kentucky, I didn't know much except I wasn't trying to stay there. If I'm honest, a part of me was chasing a boy I thought I loved. I foolishly believed that proximity could make him love me back. I was so green when I moved into that one-room efficiency apartment on the South Side of Chicago. And for most of the time I was there, I was broke. I had relationships with men that didn't serve me well and regularly reopened my wounds of rejection and abandonment. Right there on 75th and South Shore Drive I had what would be the first of many crises of faith. I would also learn that racism and misogynoir had never been location specific. Yet if I had to do it all again, I would have still packed up all my things and moved.

Chicago was waiting to grow me up. The city taught me that not everyone puts sugar on their grits, an appalling revelation for sure. It taught me that there is a kind of wind that, if you are not properly clothed, will slice your face clean off your skull. Chicago also taught me that the word "friend" should not be easily applied to everyone you meet and that the career that pays you the most money is not always the one that keeps you full.

I don't know if I would have gotten that kind of emotional and spiritual intel had I stayed home in Louisville. Maybe not for any reason related to my hometown either. For a long time, like a petulant child, I resisted anything Louisville had to say. At the very least, it would have taken me a whole lot longer to accept the lessons if I had stayed.

It's why I recommend that every Black person live away from home for at least two years. Preferably out of state, but at least far enough away from the familiar that driving home is not always an option. Yes, life might come at you hard and fast when you aren't steps away from the comfort of home, but so do the amazing, character-building lessons.

The first thing that shows up is resiliency. I had to get incredibly innovative—and sometimes very humble—while away from home. You get creative when you don't have a ready shoulder, a familiar neighborhood, or someone else's bank account to depend on during the lean times.

Not too far behind resilience is discernment. Everyone is going to make dumb mistakes. No, maybe yours won't be catching rides with strangers to work in order to save train fare, or partying on Rainbow Beach into the wee hours of the night, but no one is immune to stumbling around in the dark, especially when you don't know where you are or where you're going (even in the light). But given those mistakes, I learned how to read people fairly quickly as a survival technique. I especially learned how to read a different breed of White folks. Issues around race looked different in Chicago from what I was used to, so by the time I left, my oyster knife was machete sharp.

Finally, leaving [insert your town here] for a little while, if nothing else, will give you clarity. The expectations of others were still an ever-present voice in my ears, but, over time, that voice dimmed to a whisper as adulting forced me to make my own decisions.

Even as I write this, I recognize that there will come a time when my sweet girl will be ready to fly away from home. Maybe that's up the street, but, knowing her, it's likely to be the other side of the world. She will be ready to chase her dreams and begin the path to her own destiny just as she's watched her mother over the years. And I will scream and cry and yell and, I hope, because of my own experience still set her free. As Black parents, our tendency is to keep our children close. We know what the world thinks of us; all the traps and snares that await us. We also know the power of community. We think we know what's best. And yet our intervention can have devastating implications for not just our babies but also for the world that needs them and their gifts. What if Martin Luther King had never left Atlanta to study in Pennsylvania and Boston? What if Malcolm X had never left Michigan and ended up in Harlem? What if Angela Davis had not left Alabama and landed in California?

To be clear: there are always valid reasons to stay. There are also really good reasons to go. And further, there are also wonderful reasons to return. The point is that we must be willing to follow the paths of our hearts. Black folks, as a collective, and in a way that cannot be easily explained, are usually doing all three things simultaneously. We stay, as we go, so we can return. Tricia Hersey, founder of The Nap Ministry, said it perfectly: "My grandmother taught me how to live in a place but not be of the place. A metaphysical escape artist. When granny Ora and millions of others fled the deep South during the Great Migration, they were building spaceships out of uncertainty and hope. A subversive move."

Whether we physically leave a place or not, Black folks are always striving to be our authentic selves; fighting for our inherent right to be human; bouncing back from the blows of systemic racism. When we want better, we go get better. This extends beyond achievement in some narrowly defined field of success. We leave because we seek joy, and we stay because of that very reason too. We desire to be relationally confident. We want to live a life plentiful in self-worth. I do think leaving—as with all retiring of comfort zones—helps facilitate this. After Chicago, I went on to live in northern New Jersey, New York City, and Philadelphia. Every step on my journey has shaped my life, informed my character, despite the hard times and places. I'm better for it—period.

21

The Right Kind of Chili

"**W**hy is there spaghetti in my chili?"

He had the audacity to look appalled. We'd only been dating a few months and I'd cooked for him a few times. Each time he seemed pleased with my skills. But this time, he stared into the bowl of dark red beans, ground meat, onions, and spices with a look of utter confusion.

"Oh, so this is what we're doing?" I said, chuckling.

"I mean, I just never seen this before."

I rolled my eyes. "You've got to get out more then."

It was his turn to roll his eyes.

I'd grown up eating chili with spaghetti in it. In fact, before moving to Chicago after undergrad I didn't know there was any other way to make it. The same way I thought everybody put butter and sugar in their grits. And I'm sure when I had my first bowl of pasta-less chili I said something similar to my then boyfriend, now husband.

"Why *isn't* there spaghetti in my chili?"

Exposure is something, right?

Black folks do things a certain way. At least that's what I'd been taught. Until I ran into Black folks who did those same things differently. Pop was always pop until I found out it was also soda or cold drank. Sugar always belonged on grits until I learned that there were Black folks who'd burn your house down if you put anything other than salt, pepper, and butter on them.

And I'm the first one to announce to anyone who will listen the ways in which Blackness isn't monolithic. There isn't one way to be Black. Yet, at the same time, I'm incredibly curious about the thread that binds those collective differences together. The thing that makes Blackness so identifiable no matter where you are in this country or the world. And Lord knows, it can't just be struggle. Our struggle cannot be the sole thing cementing our identity and linking me to other Black folks across the Diaspora.

It must be our creativity. Our capacity for reinvention. Our resilience.

Writer Tony Pickett wrote for *Nonprofit Quarterly* what many of us know as an undeniable truth:

> . . . our proven power as Black people includes the strength and resilience to meet the challenges of a world that far too often fails to love and treat us all with a full measure of equality and respect. Our unique Black spirituality, literature, art, music, food, protests, and courageous joy-filled daily lives prove one clear indisputable fact: Overcoming is what we do!

Resilience is certainly a powerful tool for our survival as Black people. It is what keeps us creating new ways to navigate our lived experiences and reinventing what Blackness is. It's kept generations of our people alive when colonization, slavery, Jim Crow, segregation, brutality, and daily dehumanization should have long killed us. But that resilience comes at a cost, right? Having to constantly overcome takes its toll on one's mental, emotional, and spiritual health. Yes, we learn. Yes, we grow. Yes, we turn water into wine and rocks into bread, but I know I'm not the only one who longs for the day when the wine and bread are plentiful without such exertion.

In fact, Black folks have to be the most resilient people on the planet. We are proficient at the "bounce back." We've written songs about it. Remember what McFadden & Whitehead told us in the late seventies? "Ain't no stopping us now, we're on the move. . . ." Black folks are masters at turning pain into purpose. Turning trauma into triumph. For over a century, Black preachers have been using these same kinds of alliterations to keep us . . . well . . . alive. We push and press on. We work and wrestle and worship our way to some semblance of progress despite White supremacy's chokehold on our humanity.

In fact, we've gotten so good at fighting our way back that we, the collective we, tend to Flo-Jo hurdle our way over pain completely. We bypass the pain. *Because* we know we need to get to the other side, *because* we know that we have jobs to do and kids to feed, and maybe even *because* some of us don't want to end up in jail, we often choose to skip the pain altogether. We bypass the pain, bulldoze our way through our hurt, harm, and heartache, and—dare I say it—end up worse off emotionally and spiritually.

Some of us have stopped feeling to survive. We tell lies about what hurts because lies help us live another day in a world that too often wants us dead. But I often wonder if that kind of resilience is so expected of us that it's become less of a survival mechanism for our benefit and more of a way for those who hate us to continue beating up our bodies and souls. I'm reminded of the recent study that blew the lid off of the racial bias of doctors in assessing pain in Black people. In short, they believe, based on racist stereotyping, that we can take more pain, that our tolerance is higher. And so we are left to hurt and bleed. Our systems (health, political, social, religious, et cetera) hurt us and then gaslight us into believing that we aren't *really* that hurt.

This is probably why some Black folks gravitate to religion. The promise of a "by-and-by" or a "great getting-up morning" is appealing when you spend your life bobbing and weaving the hits of life. On the flip side, maybe that's always why capitalism—with all its power to turn empathy into greed—is a draw. The emphasis on "bags" and other material trappings is pervasive in parts of our art and lifestyle representations. The falsehood of "bootstrap" and "make it happen" philosophies seems to have perverted the natural and spiritual resilience of us as a people.

So where is the sweet spot? How do we recognize our resilience as a driver of our creativity and the foundation of our survival, while remaining open to the idea that we are inherently worthy, that Whiteness and its systems are not the center or a standard we need to aspire to? How do we simultaneously amplify our specific capacity for overcoming without it being an absolute expectation because we are Black and not just because we are human?

I keep coming back to joy. It not only uplifts, but it's also a leveler. It's a motivation that exists outside of the struggle. When

I do something because it brings me joy and not solely because it's the way it's supposed to be or the way I'm told Black folks are supposed to be, then something shifts inside me. An internal acceptance is born. The experience of joy—in all the myriad of forms it can take—allows me to harness all of my identity and all of the intersections that come with that identity and choose what will manifest in my life. When joy (and love and peace) is my motivation, I'm blessed with not just the creativity and capacity for reinvention that my "bounce back" provides but also the ultimate liberation—to exist outside of the boxes as I see fit. So that singular, defining thread of Blackness *is* the way we express our creativity, the way we are able to regularly reinvent ourselves, and our resilience in the face of enormous adversity. But it is also the intrinsic nature of our undeniable joy.

So whether it's a Kentucky grandmama who figured out that adding spaghetti to chili could stretch it a bit or the person who rightfully first thought that the grainy texture of grits needed the sweetness of sugar to balance it out, we are always innovating.

Maybe that's really how Black joy shows up. Maybe that's the "magic" we both claim and resist. Maybe it's our resilience wrapped in joy that is the fast track to liberation we are all looking for. And I'd submit that it's the determined pursuit of joy and *not* the struggle, not the capacity for resilience, that gives us the ability to see wine when there's only water. The ability to operate as if it's bread on the table even when we know it's rocks. The ability to live and laugh and love and demand our humanity be respected when this world tells us we ought to just lie down and die. We choose what we want to see. We been choosing.

To keep the peace, I didn't make my partner chili with spaghetti in it again. Or at least for fifteen years. Every bowl was the traditional mix of beans and ground meat (now plant based) and spices, with maybe just a little cheese and raw onions on top because that's what this Jersey boy I'd fallen in love with knew chili to be. But recently, I decided to reach back to my roots. It was time to *return* to the right way of making chili. I told him and my daughter—a Philly girl through and through—that I was going to make them some "Kentucky Chili" and they were going to have to deal. My baby girl was skeptical.

"Mommy, why is there spaghetti in the chili?"

Not this again.

"Because that's the way Nanny used to make it for Mommy."

She shrugged her shoulders and went back to her LEGOs. I suppose she is young enough to be open to something different. Plus, she thinks Nanny can do no wrong, so there's that.

Hubby just laughed as he devoured his bowl.

"Oh, so this is what we're doing?" he said.

Yes, sir.

22

If You Come to the Cookout,
Don't Stay

When people show you who they are, believe them.

—Maya Angelou

I was the managing editor at a religious publishing house for nearly two years. I was also only one of maybe two Black people in a management position at the organization. So, of course I dealt with all that comes with being a Black woman in a position of authority in an environment that celebrated patriarchy and homogeneity. Racial microaggressions were inevitable. Racial bias was regularly on display. However, one of the biggest challenges I faced was the fact that church folks, in general, can tend to cover all manner of foolishness with smiles and niceties. I certainly wasn't unfamiliar with that. In the Black church community, it was called being nice-nasty. But when racism is covered in gooey nice-nastiness, it's a whole new ball game. In fact, it's so disorienting that, if we aren't careful, we might find ourselves making excuses or exceptions for White folks who have draped their racism in piety and bogus ignorance. Pretending that they didn't know that what they said would be hurtful or, as Black folks might say, throwing rocks and hiding their hands.

This truth became wildly apparent one day as I walked into the office and into our small break room. The company was housed in an older building, probably built in the late sixties, and the room still had Formica counters, paneled walls, and heavy, dark wood cabinets. I was there making some coffee when one of my colleagues, an older White man who was at least sixty years old, came in. I'm not a morning person, but back then I was still trying to be. So I spoke.

"Hey there. Good morning. How are you doing?"

My co-worker said, "I'm doing well. How are you?"

Now, by that point in my life, I'd decided to stop lying to people when they asked me this. I know many might have answered with, "I'm fine," or, "I'm good," just moved on. And while I don't ever want to overshare, I also don't like to lie about where I am. I keep it vague with only a slight nod toward the truth of my heart. That morning was a tough one for me, so I responded with, "I'm hanging in there."

"Well, at least you're not hanging from a noose," he said.

It was truly a record scratch moment. You could've heard a pin drop. His response floored me. This man must have gathered all the audacity available to White men that day.

My heart was racing and tears started to form in the backs of my eyes. I did not know what to do. But apparently he did. Because of course when you've just conjured up an image of lynching to respond to a Black woman's casual mention of her state of mind, the only thing to do is mosey on back to your office. Totally a Jesus move, right?

On the other hand, I was stunned into silence. I grabbed my mug, went into my office, and closed the door. If anyone walked by my office in that moment, I'm fairly sure they saw the smoke seeping out from the bottom of my door. What they didn't see was me, pacing the floor as anger had me bursting at the seams. I had done everything I could in that space to balance being my unapologetically Black self with the awareness of where I was. I'd tried to see these people as individual human beings with their own paths and experiences—much in the same way I wanted to be seen. You know, "do unto others" and whatnot. I could've easily walked into that organization with the perspective that "these are White folks. White evangelicals. I know exactly what they are about." And at that juncture, maybe I should have. Because that man's statement told me everything I needed to know about the true nature of the culture where I worked. It also got me thinking about my engagements with White folks in general. I couldn't help but wonder if our deaths, collective or individual, are never far from their subconscious as a possibility—or potentially as a necessity even when they claim the best of motives.

In nearly every single instance in my life, I've had to approach my dealings with White folks with a healthy amount of caution. Even with those I may call friends, boundaries are necessary. This is mostly because, if they have not done the hard work of becoming antiracist, of really digging up and interrogating what they believe and have been taught, then at some point something absurd is going to come out of their mouths or appear in their actions. And it's going to hurt me. Whether I expect it or not, whether I'm surprised by it or not, it's still going to hurt. It's why any White folks who would call me friend subconsciously know that, even if they are invited to the proverbial cookout, there are no cookies waiting to celebrate their "bravery" in choosing to come and they shouldn't stay too long.

I gathered myself enough to have a conversation with my co-worker a couple of days later. And of course, he had "absolutely no idea" what I was talking about.

"Oh, I didn't really mean it that way.

"Oh, I didn't even think about that."

But interestingly enough, the discussion took a turn into a diatribe (or explanation or excuse) that included him talking about his encounter with another Black woman ten years earlier. A woman whose "anger" startled him and apparently was something he couldn't get over. He tried to link his engagement with that person to the one he was having with me and it made no sense whatsoever.

I left the company shortly after that experience. I had to. The place had been unmasked. When one racist aspect of an environment is revealed, you begin to see it everywhere. I told my boss, another White man, before I quit that there was no joy left. I said it was a psychologically and spiritually hostile environment and I couldn't serve the work I did there because the organization didn't have the capacity to serve me. Of course, he too had "no idea" what I was talking about.

Setting boundaries is a core piece of being resilient. We bounce back because we have figured out just how far we will let a thing go. Setting boundaries with White folks is necessary if for no other reason than they too have their own generational traumas around race to reckon with. Even those with the best intentions will often find themselves navigating an environment with Black folks and bringing that underlying sense of superiority to the encounter. This is how we can have allies—people who define themselves as progressive—still centering themselves in our movements, telling Black folks how to protest and when. It's how we can still see White women who center their needs within the larger feminist movement under the guise of "we're all women" without understanding the intersectional nature of the misogyny that Black and Brown women face. Boundaries are too often not a thing that White people respect when set by Black folks. Maybe it's residue from the 1857 *Dred Scott* Supreme Court decision that said that Black folks "had no rights which the white man was bound to respect." I suspect the perspective is much deeper, though.

Many White folks are not interested in hearing us tell them no or "you cannot come to this place" or "this is not a space for you." The colonizer mentality that seeps up through the bloodline says, *No, I can go anywhere. I can do anything. I can take up space.* When Black folks begin to take up space and to take ownership of the things that are inherently ours as human beings— our joy, peace, and love specifically—things suddenly become complicated or problematic.

> When it comes to racial justice, whatever hope I possess is not found in the potential for more white allies. My hope is in blackness. In knowing that we will never stop demanding our freedom.
>
> —author and activist Austin Channing Brown

Black joy is never without its boundaries. As wild as I want my joy to fly, it doesn't mean just anyone can experience it with me. Not because I'm trying to be mean. Not even for any kind of revenge. Chiefly because even the generational representation of White folks can taint the purity of the experience. They might be invited to the cookout, but they will never be able to access the meaning behind why Mama puts neck bones in her greens. Standing firm in my identity, in my Blackness, means having space to be without disruption. And losing people who don't understand that will always be better than losing myself.

23

Cover Me

cover [kuhv er]—to place something over, as for protection, concealment, or warmth; to envelop; to offset
(an outlay or liability)

When my friend sent me the picture, I was astonished.
"When was this taken?" I asked.

"I'm not sure. I think it was at the end of the show. I thought
it was beautiful and you'd want to have it."

I kept staring at it. Me, dressed in all white (it was an all-
white party and concert), locs barely grazing my shoulders,
flower pinned above my ear, eyes bright with excitement, and a
smile as wide as the ocean. I was twenty-eight years old and I'm
sure I hadn't smiled that wide in a picture since seventh grade.
Ever since D.W. told me my gums were too big and black. Since
R.M. said I looked like a neighing horse when I smiled.

I spent most of my single, dating years hiding myself. Only
allowing the men I dated to see parts of me. The parts I thought
were my best. The parts I thought they would be most attracted

to according to the prevailing, Eurocentric beauty standards of the day. The parts that were most acceptable. I liked my eyes but hated my wide mouth. So I blinked a lot and smiled very little. But this wasn't just about my physical attributes. It extended to my emotional and spiritual self as well. I was only comfortable with showing the acceptable parts of me—how smart I was (but not too smart), how nice I was (even to my own detriment)— because I thought if they really got to know Tracey in her entirety, I wouldn't be wanted. I would be rejected. I was sure they'd find the real me too weird or too something or another (as if a blinking, no-smiling half person is not weird enough). And most of the time, I *was* rejected. The men I drew never got the me I showed them. And after much healing work, I now wonder if those rejections had more to do with the parts of me they didn't get a chance to see than the parts that they did. Wholeness is always more desirable.

By the time I met someone who was willing to unveil my camouflage and I got married, things changed dramatically. Not because I necessarily wanted them to—I still preferred my disguises. Mostly because marriage—really any partnership where the parties are fully invested—doesn't afford you the chance to hide. Your mask, no matter how well adhered, eventually wears off as the highs and lows of life together begin to reveal your real self. You are now exposed and naked before your mate daily. Not just physically but, again, also emotionally and spiritually. All of the beautiful, broken, ugly, wonderful, wretched parts of your being are brought to their attention and, maybe most important, yours.

That's why I love when the word "cover" is used to describe how partners should treat each other. It reminds me of those terribly predictable cop shows where the two officers, partners, are hiding behind a car in a shootout. One of them will inevitably say, "Cover me!" which means that the other will either go on the offensive or take the heat of oncoming fire until the first makes it to safety.

Every time my partner sees me, he is covering me from the open fire of life. Even when my exposure to the danger is a result of my own issues, he covers me. Offsets my liabilities. Demands that the world see both my beauty and brokenness through his eyes, his love.

This is what I also believe Black folks ultimately do for one another. We can't hide from one another. No, all skinfolk are *not* kinfolk. But standing vulnerable in front of one another, exposing our needs, our desires, is the only way we can ever truly see one another no matter if we rep the hood, the country, or the suburbs, whether we have SNAP cards or black cards. Because we are constantly under fire. The bullets of White supremacy steadily threaten to take us out of here. And sometimes we have to call out to our partners, our people. The ones we love and maybe even those we also deeply dislike. We have to say, "Cover me!" as we help one another race to the next rung of safety. The next step toward justice. It's true that it is risky. It's true that some have been lost. But the best way to fight has always been together.

24

Black People Invented Time Travel

Your teachers
Are all around you.
All that you perceive,
All that you experience,
All that is given to you
or taken from you,
All that you love or hate,
need or fear
Will teach you—
If you will learn.

—Octavia Butler, *Parable of the Sower*

My great-grandmother's stories were never the same but were also never different. From the time I can remember, up until she was moved into a nursing home, my family would visit Nanny on some Sundays after church. She was one of those people everyone knew. Mostly because she could spin a yarn like no one else. And maybe because Ms. Lopez on the fourth floor, as everyone in the building called her, would have the entire hallway outside her door smelling like a soul food restaurant.

It wasn't just Sundays. I was always amazed by the fact that, no matter what time of day we came to visit, no matter when or who we were with, she always had at least her silver stock pot of collard greens and a cast-iron skillet of corn bread on the stove, ready for anyone who wanted to eat. The magical part being that no matter how many people stopped by, there was always enough. I'm not sure it was just hospitality, although that certainly was part of it. More than anything, the food was a preamble. You weren't just stopping in for a second and bouncing when there was a plate waiting on you. Seconds would turn to hours as you ate and listened to her gas up her Black elder spaceship and fly you to another place and time in our ancestral narrative. While she alone was driving, she was always ready to take me soaring through time, and I was completely there for it. With me born in the seventies and coming of age in the eighties and early nineties, my world with all of its issues was extremely different from the one she grew up in. I wanted to see more.

Sunday dinner is when we'd really fly. We'd sit at her tiny dining table as she talked about growing up in Alabama or who favored who in the family or the Masons and the Eastern Stars or the goings-on at the church. As a kid, I wasn't always paying attention to the details. Most of the stories were of interest to my parents. It was the atmosphere that captured me. It was the ham hock in the greens and how the corn bread wasn't sweet. It was the smell of mothballs that slapped my face on the rare times I got to go in her bedroom. It was the Maxwell House can that she sat by her chair. The one that would make you vomit if you looked in it because Nanny chewed and spit tobacco. It was the floor-model television with the "newer" one on top. All of these images were the setup. You had to take it in before you could ride her stories into the next dimension.

Yes, my nanny was a certified time traveler. Born in 1908, she took us to the early twentieth century with her memories of sharecropper fields and the arrival of Jim Crow. Through her words, I was intentionally transported to a place where I could embody her. I watched her earn the nickname Scrap because, well, she knew how to fight and wasn't afraid to. It was surreal. Now, more than two decades after her death, my great-grandmother's stories come to me in fits and starts. Blips of memory where she is talking about her siblings and their children. About skin color as a measure of worth. In fact, what I understand about both racism and colorism in the Jim Crow, post-Reconstruction South comes just as much from me processing those stories that she told me as a child as any book I've studied.

Black folks have been time-traveling for a very long time. Our rocket ships aren't made of wood or steel. They are made of blood and memory. Of words that distill reality into fantasy so survival makes sense. Of both consciousness and the stuff that lies just beneath it. And as griots do, like my nanny did, the stories are both the same and different every time they are told. Simply because the storytellers are usually telling it from an alternate angle each time. A distinct point of view. The first-person pain might show up on Monday with its grasp on the gut of a matter. The third-person observations will swing by on Friday, concerned only with the particularities. And of course, second-person is for Sundays. That's when those who are listening are truly invited in. We get that good preachin'. The kind that soothes and convicts at the same time. It's like they know the part you need to hear.

So at seven years old, I may have needed to hear about what it was like for Nanny to live on a sharecropping farm and still manage to find ways to play. When I was eleven, that same story might have just been a litany of all the chores she had to do before the sun rose. Or my mom may have needed a different narrative in order to make sense of what it meant to give birth at nineteen. It wasn't so much that the story changed. It was more that it shifted to meet the need of the person who was taking the ride. The person who was traveling with Nanny. She drove that ship—more wondrously than consciously—in the direction that the person who was listening had to go.

Black folks can tell a story fifteen different ways because there's always fifteen different paths. There's always fifteen different ways to take an experience in; to process it. This is a necessary survival mechanism. One I do not resent even a little bit. I know it's popular nowadays to talk about wanting Black people to aspire to more than survival. Clearly, I believe that. But we also must never despise the stories; the ways in which we and our ancestors have survived. We all have to survive first before we can thrive. As Octavia Butler wrote, "That's all anybody can do right now. Live. Hold out. Survive. I don't know whether good times are coming back again. But I know that won't matter if we don't survive these times."

By necessity, Black folks have pierced the veil of time by crafting messages that not only take us back and forth across eternity but also transcend multiple generations. This is as true today in the twenty-first century as it was in 1980, as in 1960, and as in 1910. Storytelling for us isn't just a bunch of words someone is saying or writing. It's a transaction. It's an exchange of energy and insight. I was drawn to Nanny's stories because of what I knew and didn't yet know I was getting.

In any science fiction story, the first rule of time travel is to not change a thing. Nanny, like the elders before and after her, was masterful at traveling through time without shifting the whole universe in the process. Time travel was and is simply an act of healing. Whether we change things or not, whether our present lives shift one iota, there's something about sitting in the memory of joy and love and, yes, even pain. There's something about it that makes us stronger.

25

Accepting the Nonacceptance

> I am not tragically colored. There is no great sorrow
> dammed up in my soul, nor lurking behind my eyes. I
> do not mind at all. I do not belong to the sobbing school
> of Negrohood who hold that nature somehow has given
> them a lowdown dirty deal and whose feelings are all
> hurt about it. Even in the helter-skelter skirmish that
> is my life, I have seen that the world is to the strong
> regardless of a little pigmentation more or less. No, I do
> not weep at the world—I am too busy sharpening my
> oyster knife.
>
> —Zora Neale Hurston, *Dust Tracks on a Road*

I sat on the cappuccino-colored couch listening to him berate me. It wasn't the first time I'd heard how worthless I was, how incompatible we were, how there were so many others who would love to be in my position. I wanted to leave. To walk away from the awfulness of the words that bounced around the room. But my feet were lead. Something held me there. Kept me stuck. Forced me to sit and soak in the indignities. I waited. For him to tire. For God to maybe switch the levers of his conscience. He was always apologetic, in the end. So I waited.

But this time was different. He stood above me as I remained rigidly seated on the edge of the sofa. Ironically, on edge is where I'd become comfortable since we'd started dating.

"Get out!"

I wasn't sure I'd heard him correctly. He'd never actually put me out before. Sure, he'd forced me to sleep on his couch when his bed was off-limits, but he'd never banished me.

"Are you hard of hearing too?"

"Why?"

That wasn't the question I really wanted to ask. I didn't really care why. In fact, as I said, I wanted to leave. I just didn't want *him* to want me to leave.

During the few years we dated off and on, my life felt like one very long, very bad B movie. The kind where the viewer wants to throw something at the main character for being so stupid; for making the wrong choice when the right one seems so obvious. Yet it never occurred to me until many years after that relationship had ended to trace my reluctance to putting my own emotional well-being first back to a desperation for acceptance I had learned back in childhood.

As a child, and even well into my adulthood, I wondered why my biological father didn't want me, why he never fought to be able to see me. Of course, I now know that the story of my birth and the subsequent years is a complicated narrative that didn't have much to do with any direct dismissal of me. But an eight- or eleven- or seventeen-year-old can't often process nuance well. I just held on to my sorrow. Kept it inside and, I think, unknowingly vowed that whenever I had an opportunity to gain the love and acceptance I so fiercely wanted from someone, I would try to make them stay.

I was reminded recently that I've done this in my friendships. I have a sign on the tiny meditation altar I have in my office that says: *Create the Stories You Wish Existed.* For the longest time, I thought of this as an admonition to keep pushing myself as a writer. But the truth is, this phrase wasn't just a directive for my work. It was an unconscious mandate for a mind that likes to create narratives that aren't true and, frankly, center me unnecessarily. It's the story I told myself when I hadn't heard from a friend in a while. The story that said they weren't speaking to me because of the last thing I said to them. Then I'd fall all Alice-like down the proverbial rabbit hole, dissecting every conversation we'd had in the last decade. My friend was most likely busy. Or overwhelmed with some other part of their life. Their disconnection from me might have been for any number of reasons other than something that had to do with me, and really, I just needed to chill.

I soon learned that it was time to create new stories, build new narratives. Ones that weren't such a distraction from what I was actually supposed to be thinking about. And if, on the off chance, I did learn that the silence from a friend was because of some misunderstanding, I could deal with it, one human to another, but not from some frenzied place of low self-value or -worth.

In romantic relationships, I found that I did whatever I needed to make men stay. Even to my own detriment. I equated their presence with acceptance and their absence with rejection. I wrenched myself into whatever shape they told me to be. And in most cases, these men still left. In every case, that sent me spiraling. I'm now married and, despite having healed some of those desperate places, there are still times when I find myself tightening my emotional grip on my partner until he can't breathe. Needing reassurance—clear evidence—that he has accepted me even almost two decades later. Fear of abandonment regularly tempting me to make him pay for the hurt my body remembers as rejection by my biological father.

Gratefully, I came to a point where I had to confront this. I had to ask myself: What parts of me have been so fractured that I would continue to seek people's acceptance outside of myself—not out of the natural, human need for connection but out of a deeper void? A chasm that revealed my earliest traumas and my lack of healing in those areas. Why couldn't I see my inherent worth and lead with that in every encounter?

And it wasn't just in my relationships. Twenty years ago, I worked in sales and marketing for a very buttoned-up Fortune 100 company that had a very conservative (read: White) corporate culture. I'm surprised I don't have significant injury to my back the way I'd bend and contort myself to the standards of Whiteness that were set before me as the only way to climb some ladder of success I'd been told about but that only seemed to exist as a metaphor. I straightened my hair, perfected my White voice, wore navy blue power suits, and did all the things. Ludmila Leiva wrote about this in her essay "Be Your Authentic Self at Work—but Only If You're White":

Professionalism has long been a synonym for whiteness, especially given that dreadlocks and other natural Black hairstyles, the use of Spanglish, Chicano English, or African American

Vernacular English (AAVE), and many other non-white cultural signifiers are routinely flagged as inappropriate in the workplace. Basically, for many people of color, showing up "authentically" in the workplace isn't really an option. Doing so may risk you being deemed unprofessional.

For me, none of the ways I held myself back from who I was, the ways I diminished myself, ever filled me up. None of it gave me the authentic acceptance I was looking for. Probably because none of it was authentic to me. So I stopped bending. I dyed my hair Dolly Parton blond and put it in cornrows. Less than a month later, I was offered a severance package and laid off.

On the minor end of the spectrum, we tone down the way we speak, change the texture of our hair, choose mannerisms that are more "appealing to the mainstream" not because we want to—I'm a firm believer in doing what you want—but because we feel like we have to. On the extreme, we bleach our skin and vote for fascists, and at the end of it all they still don't like our Black asses. We're still not truly accepted.

One of the most powerful things Black folks can do is embrace our nonacceptance. This is where Black joy thrives. This is what resilience truly looks like. We know the story of how race as a construct came to be. But there is a pride that comes from watching what we did with it. When we eschew the original motives for these racial markers and decide to no longer center Whiteness as the standard by which we will live, we unlock something dazzling. We Black. And each individual who is of African descent is their own brand of Black. No, we didn't choose this identity. Particularly if we are descendants of the enslaved, we took that label, an identity given to demean and brutalize us, and created a whole people and culture. That's just what we do. You hand us the fatback of a pig and we use it to make savory greens. You hand us a fledgling radio station and we turn it into a media empire. You hand a Black man in prison a double life sentence and a bedpan and he might just make some baked macaroni and cheese out of it. (True story. Well, at least as true as stories are on Instagram.)

We are alchemists. So our ability to transform our lived experiences—even the ones plagued by trauma—is the very reason why we should internalize our acceptance and release ourselves from any obligation to be something other than who we are, individually and collectively.

I always want to stay clear of monolithic language when describing the Black experience. At the same time, I can't help but revere the fact that there are some really glorious distinctions and demonstrations of Blackness that show up all across the Diaspora. And the full acceptance of that Blackness as a category all its own and not the shadow side of Whiteness or some lesser subsection is critical to me. I suggest we lean into the fact that society doesn't fully accept us. Decide that cultural acceptance while it has its privileges doesn't ultimately serve us. It keeps us from our natural evolution as we twist ourselves into an image that was never ours to hold.

Accepting ourselves frees us up to create pockets of joy where our Blackness is not treated as a burden because of our labor but a blessing deserving of being focalized.

I'm not suggesting at all that we deny or somehow believe ourselves to be above our identity. Actually, the opposite. We

Black. We can be Black. In a myriad of ways, with a myriad of meanings. Yes, we didn't create the construct of race, but since it's here, and is the foundation of how we must navigate this world, we will choose it.

When we choose Blackness—which as I've stated here might mean choosing unacceptance—it's glorious. When we decide to wrap our arms tight around what Blackness means to us, hold it, love it, and yes, even interrogate it, then we snatch that construct out of the hands of those who thought they had the power to use it to make us inferior. We say, "Give me that Blackness and let me show you what I will do with it. Let me roll it between my fingers and in my mind. Let me set your intentions on fire and create something new. Something that, as colonizers, you'll desperately want later on. Let me create the baseline that holds your national melody together. I see you coming to steal it. But as soon as you do, I'll flip it again and you will need to overhaul your systems just to catch up. I will turn my gospel into blues into jazz into r and b into rock into funk into disco into hip-hop. You'll look back over entire industries and when you remove the mask you'll only see our joy behind the creativity. We will lean into your non-acceptance, no matter how much it hurts, because deep down we know that on your best day you could never."

We're not sad if you don't like or love us. We have our oyster knives.

. . . as *restoration*

IF THE MEANS IS JOY,
THE END MUST BE OUR HEALING

MAY JOY FREE YOU TO

- *Remember your first loves*
- *See and be seen*
- *Honor the expansiveness of time*
- *Hold fast to your wonder*
- *Declare yourself healed and free*

26

You

I fell in love with you for the first time at fourteen. I proceeded
to love you for the next ten years.

My present inclination is to add the phrase "off and on," but
the deep down, ugly beautiful truth is that there was never an
"off." There were only the times you had a girlfriend. The times
when I had a man. And the times in between when we called each
other friend but fearfully longed to feel the intensity of those
days when we'd kiss and touch on the twin bed in the room you
shared with your brother.

Before you, I'd had many crushes. Boys I liked. Boys I'd sneak
and call on the phone when my parents weren't home.

"You hang up."

"No, you hang up first."

But that day by the lockers, in my freshman year, the month
I got my first asymmetric haircut, the week I'd carefully planned
the black creased pants, white oxford button-down, and red
turtleneck I'd wear with the goldish herringbone chain peeking

out the top, something in the pit of my stomach revealed a heart triggered. I tried to play it cool. Tried to ignore the rumblings of affection. Snuck glances of you even as I tried to steady the books in my hands. It would take another couple of months for us to actually talk, and another couple before we'd decide that maybe we could *talk* talk.

We were kids. Broken by adults who didn't know we were always listening. Always wanting to be seen but succumbing to all the things teenagers do. I've been told that love requires a witness. Well, we didn't have many of those. I remember your friends asking you why you "messed with" me. I wasn't the girl guys fought over or lied about. I didn't look like Nia Long and Lisa Bonet or any of the girls in the Al B. Sure! videos. I hadn't come into my face yet. Which only means I didn't realize the beauty that stared back at me in the mirror because it was obscured by the images of the day that had not yet said a regular Brown, Kentucky girl with thick, 4B hair, wide-set eyes, and a gummy smile could hold any allure. My own voice of affirmation was drowned out by the middle school taunts of, "Lionhead!" and, "Gumby!" and, "Horsey!" I'd actually stopped smiling altogether just three years before when I learned my smile provoked my torment.

But you didn't care about all that, did you? I'd like to think that you saw through whatever imperfections preoccupied me at the time. That my beauty was evident to you in ways I wouldn't see for another fifteen years, long after you left my life. The idea that someone could like me, could want to spend time with me even if under cover, was intoxicating. I held no regret for bending the strict rules of my hyper-religious parents because the hunger for your friendship, for the potential of safety that dangled like a carrot from the memory of our first kisses, kept me enchanted.

A sunny-colored school bus with puke green seats. A field trip to some place or another. Maybe the convention center? The background is blurred because all I could see was you. With the obligatory fresh, box haircut of every Black teen boy in Jefferson County, the deep-set almond eyes and round wire-framed glasses, you rode the same bus as me on this trip. Of course I thought you'd want to sit with your boys so you all could play the dozens and fling worn-out insults about one another's mamas. My insides twisted themselves into knots when your flattop cracked the surface of the seat that blocked the bus stairs and you walked down the aisle. My heart burst when, instead of taking your expected post, you sat down next to me.

No one had done that before.

I'd worn my acid-washed blue jean skirt hoping you'd notice. You did. You walked around the convention center—was that where we were? I really can't remember—with me. You held my hand.

No one had done that before.

Eventually, you gave me a ring. A tiny, fake copper ring that was supposed to be a promise of something special between us. I wore it like it was the Hope diamond. More than just a symbol of our burgeoning relationship, I held it up as evidence that I was worthy. That I had value. That somebody, when they said my name, thought me to be more than smart. More than cool. More than just the sidekick of the really fly chicks. Somebody worth loving.

Years of therapy would later undo this habit of gauging my

worth by what somebody else says or does. At fifteen, though, it felt like a reasonable conclusion. But of course, the stories I made up in my head about the depth of this love I thought we had meant that when I learned you'd shared your affections with another girl I tossed that ring on the lunch table next to your rectangle pizza and in front of all of your boys. Then, I walked away.

At least for a little while.

I want all of this to be true. I know that much of it is. But being loved back then—even the flighty, unsure-of-itself love of a teen boy—felt so wonderfully foreign, so unattainable, that I often wonder if my brain made these stories up. If the hopes and dreams of just being loved by someone had skewed reality. If I made up this love out of a need to fill the gaping hole in my soul. I suppose only 1992 will know.

You'd come back around a few more times. The first being that time on the senior boat ride. Me with my neon green Cross Colours shorts and white net shirt with the white tank top underneath. My hair growing out from the junior year T-Boz cut. You with the plaid jams and quiet calm as you stood behind me at the railing and whispered in my ear. The hairs on my neck and arms reaching for the moon that seemed to hover just above us. I'd just broken up with my first "official" boyfriend. The one who had my parents' stamp of approval. The first one I'd actually brought to the house. He'd done me dirty and caused me to miss prom—the same prom where you'd said you would drop your date to go with me if my parents allowed it. They didn't, but your offer affirmed me and so I reveled in your sweet kisses as the boat bounced along the Ohio River. In a few months we were going off to college. We were going to meet other people. Dance a new dance with adulthood and all that comes with that. So I savored the moment, pushed the uncertainty deep down, and wished for seventeen to last forever.

There's something about the way we got down in the early to mid-nineties. Prince had it right. The parties were galactic. It was just like it was 1999. Which still felt like a long ways off. There was still an innocence, a naïveté, among most of the other young, Black twentysomethings I knew, tempered by just enough awareness of how the world was changing. We'd dumped our pagers and gotten our first cell phones with the free nights and weekends plans. We'd chosen majors and then second-guessed our choices because tech was rising, the bubble had not yet burst, and who cares about dreams of writing when there was money to be made in sales. You liked to cook. Told me one day you'd like to become a chef. Which was cool because I liked to eat. It never occurred to me to think about whether you could/would consume my dreams in the same way. If I wanted to write, then maybe you'd grow into loving to read. I was willing to accept that potential as fact. Something Black girls in love are wont to do.

Nevertheless, it was like all of us back then knew we were up against a clock. Like it could only be "all about the benjamins" but for a hot second. As I percolated myself into oblivion in a club I was just old enough to be in, the news hit about Tupac. The following year, my first, post-undergrad, living in Chicago, Biggie was gone. Maybe that should have been our clue. But we held on desperately to whatever joy we could conjure from our New Jack aspirations and bottles of MD 20/20. We were only allowed our abeyance in spurts, but we rode that thing until the wheels fell off. And they did.

"You need to stop calling him! He's my man! And I'm having his baby!"

When your first love's first love calls you and spits the hard truths, it's enough to make you sink into the floor. That should have been it. And it was. Until I found myself a bit saucy after a party and riding thirty minutes to your campus with my roommate. I needed a place to crash and you rarely said no to me. Even when you wanted to. When you should have.

I always thought I'd lose my virginity to you. I'd hoped for it. Planned for it. Created elaborate narratives in my mind about how it would go down. But it wasn't you, was it? And that wasn't the only story I made up. I also thought we'd one day find our way back to each other. Get married. Have some kids. You'd already started that, though. One child, then another. Not with me. Not ever with me.

The last time I saw you, you'd come to visit me in Chicago. I was ready then. I thought I could counter whatever you had going on at home, whoever you were with, with a ten-year-old love and friendship wrapped in an exciting new life I was forging for myself as the Kentucky girl in the big city. And maybe that's why you stayed out that night. You were supposed to hang out with some male friends of mine for only a few hours while I took care of something with a girlfriend of mine. I waited for you to come back so I could finally profess my love and give myself to you. I had South Side courage now. I could tell you how I felt and what I wanted. But you didn't come back until morning. And by then, my courage was but a minuscule thing thrown into the corner of my one-bedroom apartment in favor of a fierce anger that would simmer for a few years before being quenched by other loves.

That first love had finally and officially faded to black. A solemn and nostalgic voice at the end of the prototypical nineties movie. Only it wasn't a script. It was real; as real as any story I could tell. My love for you is now but a decade-long footnote in nearly a half-century of stories. That thing we replaced with new healthier, grown-up loves. A husband. A wife. Children and careers. Grief and loss. And so many, many years.

But I do wish I knew at the time what it truly meant to savor those moments. Not just to live them one by one, moving from one event to the next. But to take the joy into my body and hold it, letting the sensations fill those aching crevices made by trauma and life's wrecking ball. It would take another twenty years and more and more therapy to be free enough to do that. But I'm still grateful for first loves that teach us who we are and who we are not.

27

Someday It Might Snow in April:
The Healing Power of Prince

I was dreamin' when I wrote this
so sue me if I go too fast
—Prince, "1999"

O ne can dream, right?

There are just some artists whom Black folks expect to live forever. Stevie Wonder. Misty Copeland. Kehinde Wiley. Beyoncé. I don't know why. Intellectually, of course, we know that we die and so will they. But there are some whose work has such a monumental impact on both the individual and the collective that they seem immortal. These legends found a way to infuse their craft with enough of themselves that they are the joy soundtracks of our lives and our movements. They are the great translators. And maybe because of their legacy—what they leave behind for us—they, in fact, are immortal.

Prince is one of the immortal ones.

His music is seismic. Soaring high above trends and expectations, his work shifted and transformed those of us who understood it. It moved our feet, sure, but it also pricked our hearts, seared our souls, and opened our minds. It pushed and challenged us. It healed us. Because of this we feel like we know him. Like he's part of our family. And just like when a family member dies suddenly, we are devastated. We mourn him like we mourn the death of that favorite cousin who used to hold our hands while crossing the street when we were little or the auntie who used to defy our mother's orders and sneak us off to the ice-cream parlor in the park. Everything in our world stops for a moment or three as tears rain purple down our cheeks. It might be cliché to keep saying that Prince's music has been a major part of the soundtrack of our lives, but some platitudes are just freaking true. If my life were a double album, then Prince probably would have half of all the tracks. Since the day we met, he's scored some pivotal moments.

Yes, I said "met."

I suppose we shouldn't have met the way we did. I mean, it was 1984 and I was only nine. But I had a young mama who had been rocking with Prince since *Dirty Mind* and, for her, not having a babysitter was, by far, not enough of a reason to miss the theatrical debut of her favorite artist. So with store-bought Lemonheads and Boston Baked Beans in her purse, we all went to see *Purple Rain*.

"Close your eyes!" she loud-whispered at me when Prince, with a sly, sexy smirk, told Apollonia that she would have to purify herself in Lake Minnetonka and a few scenes later took her deep in another kind of way.

I didn't get it at first. I mean, I was nine. He wore leather and lace. And eyeliner. He didn't look like the sex symbols I was digging. He certainly wasn't any Ralph Tresvant (lead singer of

New Edition). But it all changed a couple of years later. I'll never forget lying on my back reading the liner notes on the *Around the World in a Day* album and being completely mesmerized by songs like "The Ladder" and "Pop Life." I remember thinking here was a man who didn't give a damn. A man who found a way to say the most powerful things in the funkiest way possible. That was attractive. And at a time when I wasn't sure if my voice mattered, or if the way I chose to speak my heart could be heard, Prince restored my confidence with every lyric and note.

There were so many more moments. *Batman* wasn't worth seeing for me until I heard "Batdance." Then there was that time in my junior year of high school when the boy I liked didn't like me back and I sob-sang "Diamonds and Pearls" until I fell asleep. And lying on the floor of my Y2K-ready Chicago apartment on New Year's Eve 1999 and watching the Purple One on pay-per-view with my then boyfriend. In fact, if I were to remove my halo and plug my mama's ears, I might have to admit that I may or may not have had songs like "Insatiable," "Do Me, Baby," "Scandalous," and "Erotic City" on regular rotation during some of the riotous seasons of my life (see: my twenties).

Although, now that I think about it, my mama took her nine-year-old to see *Purple Rain*, so I think she probably gets it.

I'm not alone, though. My friend Rainah Chambliss, a woman who'd probably categorize herself as so much more than *just* a Prince fan, has Prince to thank for her entire family: "On October 18, 1988, I saw him in concert for the first time. Outside the doors of the Spectrum in Philly is where I met the man I've been married to for 23 years. Prince introduced us. He's why my family exists and will be '4ever in My Life.'"

Prince's physical stature belied his talent and courage (I mean, this is the guy who changed his name to a symbol and sued his record label for ownership of his music). He was big in all the ways that mattered. And his words, my God, those lyrics?

Everybody's looking 4 the ladder . . .
There are thieves in the temple tonight

If I didn't know before, I know now: there is a mystic power in words. Sure, I'm a writer and an artist so *of course* I'd be drawn to them. Nah, with Prince, it was something else entirely. A transparency; a nakedness. An unwillingness to be anything but himself at every iteration of his journey. As Black people, we needed to see this even if we didn't always understand it. Even if it challenged our own internalized phobias and forced us to see the breadth and depth of who we are and who we could be as a people. Joy born from that kind of freedom of being transforms us into stronger fighters for our own rights and the rights of others. We then can weaponize it against every force in this world that tries to deny our humanity. Prince taught us that. He taught us how to take something that we love, our precious gifts, and make it matter in places we're told it shouldn't. It was the ultimate resistance strategy.

It's that authenticity that made Prince's untimely death hurt so much. And yet the legacy of his music, his immense presence as an artist and man, is why I—and the rest of the world—love him so.

Until the end of time.

28

Born to Wash Cars

I ride for small, Black businesses. Selling a T-shirt? I'm buying and wearing it. Trying to get your cleaning company off the ground? Please come scrub my tile. Got the hottest new song, story, poem, or short film releasing? Just tell me if you prefer Amazon or your website. In another life, I worked in small business and economic development at Temple University. It was literally my job to help mostly minority-owned businesses write business plans and launch/manage their companies. So imagine how I felt the day I turned the corner in my old Germantown, Philly, neighborhood and saw a lanky brother with deep amber skin holding up a sign near an open garage:

Car Wash. Shampoo. Wax. Detail.
I was born to wash cars.

I probably pressed my brakes a bit too hard. My smile was probably wider than the road I was driving on. This young brother had rented a small, nondescript garage, put up his sign, and every morning was seen passing out flyers to cars that drove by, marketing his car wash and detailing service. Amazing! But what intrigued me the most was that last line: *I was born to wash cars.*

In addition to becoming a patron of his service, every time I drove past that sign I would tear up a little. My heart was moved beyond measure at this young man's clarity. Yes, he was a burgeoning entrepreneur who I hope by now, twelve years later, has a string of car washes, but back then he was at least clear about what he was "born" to do. Sure, to the so-called Talented Tenth, to those of us with all our degrees and pedigrees, washing cars might not seem like much of a purpose to have in life. But who are we to really judge that? By whose standard have we determined what purpose looks like? If we dig deep enough, if we are willing to expose our beliefs to the light of truth, I'm sure we'll uncover just how much we've adopted the Eurocentric, capitalistic mentality that we've had to immerse ourselves in to even get half of what we define as purpose fulfilling. Oh, what a disservice we do to the notions of destiny, intention, and purpose when we assume that purpose has anything to do with one's status and station in life. This young man *was* clearly operating in his purpose—not just because of his attention to detail in cleaning cars, but also because of the lives he touched while doing it. I can imagine the relief he may have given a single mom whose car hadn't been washed in months, and how every customer's day might be lifted by his willingness to simply provide them a quality service with a smile.

The same people who'd look down on this young man as they headed out to their high-powered, stress-inducing, soul-crushing jobs are likely to be the same ones who, five, ten, or fifteen years later, will look back and wish they'd discovered what they were actually born to do. Instead of what they were told to do. Or what they thought they should do. What they believed they had to do. Or worse, what a White supremacist economic system told them would pay them the most money to do at the time.

In all the jobs I've had in my life, I've always been clear that the thing I was called to do, the one thing I'd do whether I was paid or not, is write. Part of my own healing journey has been to reconcile the very real need to eat and live in this country with the desire to pursue that dream. This young, Black brother's courage was an affirmation of sorts that I will forever hold dear.

Maybe we should all just go make our own signs. Declare our birthrights to the world and the people who run it. Let the chips fall where they may.

29

This Is My Story. This Is My Song.

I put one foot in front of the other. Let the wind whip my face into a teary submission. Tuck my hands into pockets filled with all manner of random objects—a single hoop earring, a DSLR camera battery, my child's fake tattoo stickers. This walk along the dark and gray shore in Atlantic City is so needed. Yes, it is winter and the middle of a pandemic, so the boardwalk is a ghost town. Even better. The solace makes me feel like I have the whole beach to myself. And with the exception of a few sea gulls and a homeless woman walking in tight circles about one hundred yards away, I do. This is good. I can feel the emotion bubbling just below the surface. My body is a volcano, active and preparing for eruption. I want to cry. I want to fight. I want to kick and sob and punch and wail.

Emily Bernard, in her book *Black Is the Body*, writes that "rage is a physical condition." This is true. I've held this pain in for too long. And now it's clamoring for escape. So the ocean offers me a kind of safety that I've yet to find anywhere else. It's like the watery expanse is the only place that can hold the weight of my grief, my anger, and my joy.

Now I claim my seat on the throne. Which is really just a harder-than-I-like stool in the unfamiliar kitchen of our rental. My hands are balled into fists and hovering over the keys. They are usually anxiously drawn to their homes: a s d f j k l ;. But today they resist. The waves are still crashing, only this time, on the inside. Every crest breaks upon the shores of my soul. It's totally why I run to the beach every chance I get. To grab a little bit to carry home with me. To bottle up this healing balm so I can access it when I need it. Today, though, there is conflict. My peace has found a formidable, if not recognizable, opponent. No matter how many prayers I say, meditations I do, mantras I repeat, I am contending with my sense of safety. If there is a single factor in my inability to feel the fullness of joy, it is the challenge I face daily in feeling safe and secure in my body and mind. I imagine death and harm being like that homeless woman sharing the beach with me earlier. They linger just a stone's throw away, taunting me with their presence. Walking in tight circles in the distance of my life. I'm always hyperaware of them and it's that awareness that makes living in the present moment—a tenet of joy—difficult.

More than anything, though, I wish I didn't get so angry with myself when this happens. Or, at the very least, I wish I could honor my anger. I wish I had more grace for my story. I know why I don't feel safe. I know why my body lurches at loud sounds and my skin crawls when my hypervigilant mind tells it that danger lurks. As they say, I get it honestly. And yet I want to be different. I see people who move freely and confidently across a room. They don't worry about what they can't control. They take risks—not like me, as a way to perform for my worthiness, but because, well, they just want to. I envy them. I envy the protection they must have experienced along the way that makes them feel so secure.

Finally, I type. With the ocean raging in my gut, my fingers rest on the home keys and begin plucking my emotions like a guitar. Each digit wrenches my feelings out and onto the electronic page . . .

Who Will Protect Me?

The old church folks used to call it standing on the watchtower. It's a biblical reference to Isaiah 21 where the old prophet spoke about a lookout who would stand on his "post" and watch out for the coming salvation of the people. Though probably not contextually or culturally accurate, I always imagine this lookout as a Black woman. She's standing there with her eyes peeled on the horizon. Ready to call out what she sees. Ready to protect her village, her city, with the sound of her voice. Ready to announce that "all is well" and "salvation has come" and maybe, just maybe, "you are safe."

Because that's what we do.

We look out for one another.

We stand on the watchtower and call out what we see. We stand between police officers and our children. We stand between whole governments and our people. We stand between and among and in the midst.

Except when we don't.

Where Is My Protector?

The watchers don't often reveal themselves. Which makes it hard to see them when you are not used to being protected. For many Black folks, they live in a world of watchers. Of protectors. The corner boys who look out for peaceful protestors who are confronted by racist counter-protestors. The advocates and doulas in the delivery room, making sure Mama is getting what she needs and doesn't fall victim to the maternal mortality rates that plague Black and Brown mothers. The "auntie" in the campus cafeteria who slides you an extra piece of chicken. The porch and stoop mamas who know everything that goes down in the neighborhood and have the riders on speed dial should someone cross a line. The presence of watchers and protectors in the Black community is both common and complicated. For me, they've often been like unicorns: I dream of them. And in rare moments, they seem real. But it isn't a consistent presence. In some parts of my life, they've ghosted me and that hurt. But again, it's complicated. To protect me might have meant leaving themselves exposed. Unfortunately, the tenuous position of Black folks in this society makes safety and protection a hit-or-miss proposition at best.

And still . . .

I can concede the power of my unicorns. I've glimpsed the security they provide. When I was in the hospital after giving birth to my daughter, that same sense of not being safe, the fear of death and harm, prowled my spirit heavily. Unless they were taking her for a test, I wouldn't let my child leave my sight. Her tiny body, swaddled in the standard, institutional white blanket with blue and red stripes, slept either on my chest, skin to skin, or in her plastic, hospital bassinet. The PTSD I was unaware of at the time had me imagining all manner of devastations down to a nurse stealing my baby (probably too many Lifetime movies also contributed to that) or there being some terrible mistake where she was given some other child's medicine or the name cards were switched. The reality, though, was, I was tired. Happy about my sweet baby girl making her safe arrival to this plane, but bone-tired. Drained at trying to get her to latch. Exhausted with it all.

A Black nurse from Jamaica, maybe in her late fifties, came into my room on my second day and gave me that look. If you're Black, you know the look. It was a cross between *you are one of my babies now* and *she don't know a lick of nothing*. Every time she came in, she said, "Have you slept yet?"

"No, not yet."

"Well, when are you going to sleep?"

"I don't know."

And I didn't. I tried to close my eyes. But images of the baby falling off my chest or disappearing from her crib filled my mind.

"Honey, you're going to have to rest. I know you are worried about your baby, but she'll be just fine in the nursery for a few hours."

How do you know?

This kind of fear will have you throw every rationale out the window. Whatever joy you have in a moment will be hijacked as it cranks up its motives and sends tremors through your body or horrific images to your mind—all to keep you in its grasp. Of course the chances of something bad happening were slim. Especially the way my husband shadowed every move our doctors and nurses made. But even that narrow possibility immobilized me.

By the end of day two, I was damn near hallucinating with fatigue. My nurse put her foot down. When her accent became more pronounced, I knew what was coming next.

"Let me take the baby to the nursery. I will keep an eye on her. If you don't rest, you will regret it and you'll be no good when you leave here with her tomorrow. I promise you . . . she'll be fine. She'll be good."

My nurse's hands were already on the bassinet. I don't even think telling her no would have mattered. She was looking out for me and my baby. She knew what I needed and was going to give it to me. So I let her take my baby to the nursery. And I slept and slept and slept. It was a delicious sleep. A tranquil slumber I've yet to taste again.

I awakened to Nurse Jamaica smiling so big at me.

"You want to see your baby girl now?"

Typically, joy, in all its fullness, thrives in safety. It flourishes when we are able to trust that we are safe and protected. This is true when it comes to physical safety—think: *I'm more likely to dance in the street if I know and trust that it is blocked off*—but it's even more true when it comes to emotional safety. Ellen Boeder of The Gottman Institute wrote:

> Emotional safety enables us the freedom to . . . feel increased compassion and express ourselves freely with one another. When our body and mind experience safety, our social

engagement system enables us to collaborate, listen, empathize, and connect, as well as be creative, innovative, and bold in our thinking and ideas. This has positive benefits for our relationships as well as our lives in general.

But for Black folks, both physical and emotional safety and protection can look very different. We're faced with physical violence at the hands of those who are supposed to protect and serve us. So even when I'm supposed to be enjoying tubing and sledding with my family after the first snowfall of winter, I'm also looking over my shoulder and sweating bullets when a police car with flashing lights starts to circle the park where we are having our fun.

Even more palpable is the emotional harm. The microaggressions we endure and internalize because of our hair, our build, our voice or tone or dialect; because of our relationships, our culture, who we are and how we be. We are often put into positions of having to manage White people's emotions before we even get a chance to process our own, a violation of our humanity and a demonstration of just how little empathy can exist for us. For Black women, it's an even more nuanced position to be in. The intersection of my Blackness and my identity as a woman means that the emotional harm I experience as a Black person is amplified by the internalized racism and misogynoir I encounter within my community.

Black folks take care of one another. Without a doubt. We are watchers and protectors and whistle-blowers. We've also, out of our own pain and responses to trauma, left one another exposed. Sometimes the act of self-preservation has called for it.

Sometimes the dehumanization enacted upon us has translated into acts of dehumanization against one another. This is why I'm so glad about the recent destigmatizing (and decolonization) of mental health services and therapy. Access to the myriad of healing modalities that exist means we can offset the negative impact of our socialization.

I would never want to diminish what the watchers and protectors in our communities do. They are necessary. They are an ever-present reminder of God in human form. They are our angels who show up when we least expect it to ensure that we "make it through." But what I know about Black joy is that, in many ways, our joy thrives *despite* our lack of safety. I was not protected from the sexual abuse and assault I withstood as a child and young adult. But by doing the work to heal, I can thrive no matter my story. With every heartbreaking hashtag signaling the death of another Black man or woman, boy or girl, there is the chance that it will shatter and immobilize us individually and collectively. And yet most of us still wake up each morning determined to somehow live above and beyond our bodily and emotional insecurities. The waves crash around and within us and yet we still sing our songs of resilience.

Our reality tells us that the potential for devastation is always there. The sad truth we all know as Black people is that, because of the pervasiveness of White supremacy, the presence of White folks in any area of our lives—even the ones we love—leaves us exposed to the possibility of some kind of harm. But the power of Black joy is that it is simultaneously a remedy and a soothing agent. However it manifests—through laughter, music, culture, or community—it restores that foreboding agony.

I've found safety—and ultimately joy—on the page. These words that slip from my heart through my fingertips are my cocoon. I'm enveloped in a power to fight off my demons in ways I can't otherwise. I can say what I need to, in the way that I need to, and by doing so, I'm liberated. Even if only for a moment, my fears have to fight a whole lot harder to keep me bound. The oceans I hold inside me are able to crash wild and free because I have a place to put my pain.

30

Do You Love What You Feel?

RECLAIMING BLACK TOUCH AND PLEASURE

> I touch my own skin, and it tells me that before there
> was any harm, there was miracle.
>
> —Adrienne Maree Brown

Pleasure has always confused me. It never occurred to me that this was true until about a year after my grandmother passed away of cancer. My mom had sent me a few things that belonged to her, including some of her fabulous purses. She was, like me, such a bag fiend. When the purses arrived, I opened them and allowed the scent of her to overtake me. This was what I'd been longing for. For months prior I had been trying to remember what Granny smelled like, and there it was. A mixture of one of her favorite perfumes, Chanel N°5, and the heady smoke of cigarettes. It was all her. As the scent wafted around me, the pleasure was indescribable. I was almost immediately brought back to her embrace.

The women in my family weren't overtly affectionate. I didn't receive a lot of hugs or kisses growing up. And due to my childhood sexual trauma, hugs always felt weird to me. I've grown to enjoy hugs over the last decade or so, but before that, whenever I would hug someone, especially a man, it was hard to not fear the experience turning sexual. This was true even when I'd see someone else being hugged. Sexual abuse changes your brain that way. Even to this day, I sometimes have difficulty not mentally over-sexualizing very benign encounters. So one can imagine that if hugs were problematic, the idea of pleasure, particularly physical touch, was an even bigger hurdle.

Shame was an ever-present reality for me, especially in early adulthood. Some days, I'd feel a strange mix of satisfaction and contempt when I touched myself—whether it was my breasts or sexual organs or just my own legs, arms, or face. It took me a long time to make sense of it. Yes, part of that had to do with being molested. But I also think that a huge part of it had to do with what I gleaned from growing up in the church. There was this awareness that you shouldn't touch people. Skin, whether mine or others', was off-limits. No one said it aloud and maybe it was a function of the way sexual abuse ran rampant in con-gregations, but there was a belief that touch, at any point, could be misconstrued as something sexual. This must be where the church hug came from, that weird lean we did to keep as much distance as possible between our actual bodies and the other person's. So it wasn't until I was in my late thirties that I really began to embrace full-bodied hugs that weren't sexual but were nurturing and filling.

All that said, I believe I was born a person whose love language is physical touch. I longed for affection as a little kid but, as I got older, simply adapted to both my environment and my trauma. I found other ways to be sated. To experience pleasure. Nowadays that means standing in a garden with a harvest within reach. Or finishing a project that I'm proud of. And I fight off old ways of thinking when engaging physically with my partner. The longing for the ability to embrace pleasure in all its forms is still there.

When I walked into the room, undressed, and lay down on the table, I expected the session to go as usual.

I'd chat with my acupuncturist about where I hurt—in my body and my mind—and she'd talk me through some of it while applying essential oils to particular points on my body. She'd then open her packets of needles and begin inserting them at points that aligned with where I was experiencing pain. As someone who lives with chronic pain and PTSD, I'd done this a million times before. But that day was different.

My acupuncturist rubbed my face with an essential oil blend because I'd shared with her about the intensity of sinus pressure in my head and ears. She rubbed my chest with the same oil because I'd complained of weird knots appearing and then disappearing on my body. She then began inserting needles. At first, it was fine. Normal, even, if there is such a thing for having another person inserting needles into your body.

But then, she inserted a needle in a point on my chest, near the place where one of the knots had just disappeared. That's when the volcano erupted. Emotions I didn't know I had burst from me like an explosion of wails.

I cried—no, sobbed—in a way I hadn't in a very long time. I'm sure, in hindsight, the look on my face was comical. I was overwhelmed with sorrow and grief but was totally confused as to why it surged from my body in such a way. My face was probably a mixture of emotional release and *What the hell?!* After the session, I felt as though I'd run a marathon.

I also felt a peace and calm that I'd never experienced in my life. I'd walked into the room wanting a momentary respite and left with the sensation that the trauma that had been trapped in my body was making its way out. It was mostly a feeling more than a realization, as I hadn't quite worked out what was happening in the moment.

I suppose I *should* have known that what happened that day was possible. I am the quintessential spa person. I love all kinds of bodywork services, and if my budget were unlimited I'd have several different practitioners on call daily.

One of my favorite types of bodywork is the Korean body scrub. It's certainly not for the modest. Nevertheless, I will strip down to my Garden of Eden onesie, jump on a table, and let someone scrub my body down to the white meat in a minute. I love it. My mother? Not interested. Not even a little bit. And that's fine. I do it enough for the both of us. In fact, over the last few years I've completely immersed myself in holistic methods of dealing with stress, anxiety, and physical ailments.

However, it wasn't until this surreal experience with my acupuncturist that I realized my affinity for bodywork was rooted in more than just a need for relaxation. Through therapy and deep trauma work, specifically modalities like EMDR (Eye Movement Desensitization and Reprocessing), I figured out that the nonsexual intimate touch I received from my massage therapists, acupuncturist, and others had become a way for me to heal more deeply. A way to feel safe and human in my body. A pathway for me to return to pleasure.

After that experience, I wondered if I was typical. If Black folks and Black women in particular generally struggled with the desire for touch. And especially since the COVID-19 pandemic had outright eliminated our ability to experience that kind of intimate touch, I was even more curious. Were there others like me who craved nonsexual intimate touch or who wanted to understand their resistance to pleasure? My interest led me to ask the Black women around me—including those who work in bodywork and healing professions—about their own experiences.

Annette Deigh, a licensed social worker and mental health therapist in the metro Philadelphia area, was one of the first to respond. "Perhaps non-sexual intimate touch is so significant to me because I am a black woman AND a survivor of sexual assault," Deigh told me in a message. "I cannot think of non-sexual intimate touch without thinking about how the opposite has impacted me."

She went on to say: "At times, sexual intimate touch can still be triggering for me, even years removed from my assaults and after extensive treatment and work put into my self-care regimen. So to have positive non-sexual intimate touch in the form of mind-body work, and even from the soothing hands of my loctician, is very healing for me. . . ."

Of course I get this. And I received variations of this response over and over again.

About receiving nonsexual intimate touch, Amanda Green of Philadelphia wrote that "[it] makes me feel cared for and restores my energy. It reminds me that the aches and pains I feel are real, that my body *needs* to release the tension. There's been an expectation on Black women's bodies to give or to be used for healing and not to receive healing for ourselves. We're humans who need healing touch, too."

This resonated with me. There were too many times prior to that day in my acupuncturist's office when I'd become nearly comfortable with spreading myself thin. I'd found myself speaking about the importance of self-care to others, encouraging friends and colleagues to go to therapy and "get free," investing in my dreams, business, and family and yet finding no release for myself; no place to feel human; no place for the pain to go.

In these conversations, a theme emerged: touch that humanizes and grounds us is a near necessity for many Black women. It helps to heal from traumatic experiences and counters the diminishment we experience in everyday life.

Roberta K. Timothy, an assistant lecturer of global health, ethics, and human rights at York University, suggested in her article "Grief Is a Direct Impact of Racism" that the level of racism Black people experience causes a significant amount of grief and that one way to work through that grief is to "engage in intimacy (or massage) in a safe space—to reconstruct the power and healing possibilities of safe touch and prevent you [us] holding violent materials in your body, mind and soul."

Adrienne Carwheel, a holistic health educator in Willow Grove, Pennsylvania, explained to me why touch is so powerful in general:

"Touch lets us know we are connected to those we love. Sometimes in families, touch is withheld or initiated inappropriately. Massage, acupuncture, other bodywork allows our bodies to release what we hold on to. Our bodies are so intricately made that we are wired for connection and survival. Touch taps into that, allowing the body to speak, letting go of that which doesn't serve us."

However, for Black women specifically, we seem to be particularly drawn to modalities that call for nonsexual intimate touch. Carwheel continued: "As black women, we [often choose to not] allow touch to be tainted. It simply is a means of healing."

Abeje Bandele, an esthetician based in Lexington, Kentucky, said via message: "Receiving a service helps [me and other] black women feel beautiful, important, and like the many sacrifices we make are worthwhile. We can suffer from racism, abuse, and not feeling like we're good enough, so we need that positive reinforcement to be able to go through life."

There is an even more expansive reason for this. Black women carry traumas, including our everyday encounters with misogyny, oversexualization, and racial microaggressions, and one of the ways we seek healing or a reprieve from these experiences is through nonsexual intimate touch.

As a college professor, I often face White colleagues who run the spectrum from "mildly biased" to "downright racist." I've had whole bodies of scholarship on race and gender dismissed by these individuals in conversations and meetings because the scholars behind the theories I was presenting were Black.

These kinds of interactions often sent me running to a massage therapist as I tried to figure out how to not internalize the barrage of microaggressions. I started budgeting for monthly bodywork services. Though I couldn't articulate it at the time,

I somehow knew that both relief and release were no longer optional. They were necessities.

It's not conscious. It's not even necessarily something we set out to do with any real intention unless that's the work we're unpacking. But the active need that many Black women have to be touched—and sometimes even the resistance to it, as in the case of my mother—seems to point directly to a kind of compensation for or reconciliation of historical and present-day trauma.

Bessel van der Kolk, a scholar on PTSD and author of *The Body Keeps the Score*, wrote: "Trauma victims cannot recover until they become familiar with and befriend the sensations in their bodies." It's entirely possible, then, that nonsexual intimate touch is a way for Black women who have experienced great amounts of trauma to return to our bodies in the face of overwhelming and oftentimes devastating circumstances and environments.

There's been plenty of discourse lately around the very real need for men to experience platonic touch and pleasure also. Several prominent Black male celebrities have been in our news feeds solely because of their public displays of affection and vulnerability. But there hasn't been as much discussion about the particular intersection that Black women find themselves in when it comes to desiring platonic intimate touch.

This is likely because platonic touch is assumed to be common among women. It's assumed that women are comfortable with being touched—an assumption rife with an unsaid devaluation of women's agency over and understanding of our bodies. We cannot ignore the impact that historical trauma and pervasive misogynoir has had on Black women, driving us to bodywork practitioners in droves. The truth is, daily, Black women can find themselves countering the many skewed media narratives designed to box us into stereotypes and categories that are incomplete at best.

These images vacillate between the docile, Mammy figure to the angry career climber to the oversexed man-eater. Even our little Black girls are subject to adultification—where they are perceived to be older and more mature than they are; shrinking their childhood, criminalizing their behavior, and making them vulnerable to predators.

All of this hearkens back to the ugliest parts of human history—White supremacy, more generally, and the transatlantic slave trade and colonization, in particular. Gentle touches were rare for the enslaved African woman. Or those touches were loaded with bodily concessions. Felt pleasure was not, could not, be a priority and sometimes had deadly consequences. As a result, both the dearth of and yearning for intimate, nonsexual touch was likely passed down generationally.

Maria Yellow Horse Brave Heart, PhD, conceptualized and defined historical trauma in the 1980s as "cumulative emotional and psychological wounding across generations including one's own lifespan." What this means is that the weight of the physical and psychic wounds of our ancestors, the residue of trauma, can live on in the bodies of their descendants and is compounded by present-day struggles.

So it's no wonder that many Black women like me spend a lot of time unlocking our issues around pleasure and touch while still desiring to feel worthy beyond our sexual capacities. We're frequently working to negate these images while simultaneously creating spaces where we can receive the healing touch that we need. And even before there was a Black middle class—with a modicum of discretionary income for the privilege of professional massages, bodywork services, and spa dates with the girls—there was the hairdresser.

Lori L. Tharps, co-author of *Hair Story: Untangling the Roots of Black Hair in America* and host of the *My American Meltingpot* podcast, expounds on this subject more in an email to me:

"Black women are so often perceived to be strong, tough and resilient, that they are often the last ones to receive a gentle touch. [We] . . . are overlooked when it comes to compassionate care of any type, whether that's in the medical profession or even in [our] . . . own homes where [we] . . . are too often the ones responsible for keeping the household together. Therefore, Black women are in desperate need of intimate and loving care, touch and connections because we do shoulder the burden of so much of society."

Tharps went on to share that hairstyling has always been significant for Black women as a means of connection and intimacy. She believes there is a clear relationship between the need for intimate, nonsexual touch and what could be perceived by outsiders as a preoccupation with hair.

"Historically, Black women have always experienced feelings of love and intimacy through hair grooming practices," Tharps wrote. "Dating back to pre-colonial Africa, styling someone's hair was a way to show kinship, friendship, and care. In the United States, many Black women can recall a time sitting with an elder who showed love through hairstyling practices, whether that was a fancy style for a big event or just a simple braid done before bedtime."

I remember sitting "crisscross applesauce" between the knees of my mother as she ran her thin, rat-tailed comb down the center of my head, smeared healthy helpings of Blue Magic grease in the part, and cornrowed her love onto my scalp. There was a feeling of love, protection, and security that was completely lost to me outside that space.

Consequently, when a guy I dated in college helped me take out my Janet Jackson *Poetic Justice* braids, as well as scratched and greased my scalp, you could not have told me that we weren't going to get married. We didn't, but that's another story for another essay. The point, I think, is that I deeply equated this nonsexual act of intimacy with love and felt cared for in a way I hadn't prior to then.

So yes, when I can safely say I'm post-pandemic, I will gladly once again let someone walk across my back with their bare feet. Or savor my hair braider moving her index finger along my scalp with shea butter or eco-styling gel depending on the style. Or hug my friend a little longer when sadness chooses to linger around the edges of our souls.

Knowing why I do it only makes it more resonant. Knowing only makes me more intentional about ensuring that touch and pleasure is a priority for my own restoration journey.

31

To Be Seen

> *I am an invisible man. No, I am not a spook like those who*
> *haunted Edgar Allan Poe; nor am I one of your Hollywood*
> *movie ectoplasms. I am a man of substance, of flesh and*
> *bone, fiber and liquids—and I might even be said to possess*
> *a mind. I am invisible, understand, simply because people*
> *refuse to see me.*
>
> —Ralph Ellison, *Invisible Man*

I sat in the adjunct office grading papers. Vacillating between feelings of pride at the brilliance of my more thoughtful students and amusement at the equally impressive slacking of the others. In my periphery I saw a woman walking by in the hallway, and my heart quickened.

Was that . . . ?

I suppose her heart did its own dance too, because her double take was epic. In a near moonwalk, she backed up and poked her head in the office.

"Hey there! My name is Marcella. . . ."

Our greetings were kind and professional, of course. We still needed to feel each other out. But I'm 100 percent sure the spark of recognition and relief I saw in her eyes was reflected in my own. Seeing another Black professor in our predominately White institution felt like the cure for some chronic deficiency we'd just learned to live with. Dr. Marcella McCoy-Deh and I have been friends ever since.

There's something about the safety of a Black face. The way the hyperawareness, dare I say vigilance, you carry around as a Black person is slightly, even if momentarily, abated when you spot melanin across a room devoid of it.

And I'm sure there's some commentary here on why diversity and inclusion efforts are necessary. Why the Whiteness of a place can be problematic. But I think I'm more interested in what happens in those exchanges between two Black folks who discover each other in these spaces. I'm curious about the way our bodies heal a little bit, the way our hearts vibrate with delight, when we realize we are seeing and being seen.

As I've said, I spent many years preoccupied with being seen. Wanting to know that I had value in very external ways. That meant every aspect of my life—dating, relationships, writing, parenting—had a performative element to it. Most of my lived experiences didn't teach me that I had inherent worth. In fact, I was taught that my value was solely dependent on what I could achieve.

The biggest challenge, however, was the realization that those same performative drives were heightened when I was in all-White spaces. Because they had to be. I'd grown up in the era of "Black folks have to be twice as good to get half as much." I knew what I wanted. I'd always been ambitious. So in order to succeed in these spaces—whether in corporate America, nonprofit admin-istration, publishing, or academia—I continued to, as author and researcher Brené Brown says, "hustle for my worthiness." Doing way more than the average White person in the same or a similar position. In fact, whereas mediocrity was, to a certain extent, allowed and accepted in their hierarchy, it was absolutely a deal breaker for me. It's the dark side of Black excellence. In an effort to be the best, I had to always appear unbreakable. Working and living in these contexts turned me into a machine, which, in a way, was its own subtle dehumanization.

This desire to be seen came from always feeling like I was in a state of flux, and the assumption that recognition would firmly plant me on the positive side of all that I was striving for. I'd lived in the tension of trauma and triumph, of victim and victor, for so long that I believed if someone could truly know me, truly see me as worthy of whatever I was seeking in that moment—attention, affection, recognition, celebration—then I could finally become who I was supposed to be. At least I thought so. I would later learn that everything I needed was already within. That I didn't have to earn my worth. That I was inherently valuable. But at the time, those words sounded like the bootleg affirmations of some fake internet guru. And even if I did believe it, those words didn't acknowledge or validate the reality in which I was living. I was a Black girl, in mostly White spaces, trying to eat. Trying to grow. Trying to accomplish my purpose. Every day I set foot outside my door, I was the embodiment of the duality that W. E. B. Du Bois famously spoke about in his book *The Souls of Black Folk*: "One ever feels his twoness,—an American, a Negro; two souls, two thoughts, two unreconciled strivings; two warring ideals in one dark body, whose dogged strength alone keeps it from being torn asunder."

I was a version of the narrator pontificating in Ellison's *Invisible Man*. In some ways, I was Florens from Morrison's *A Mercy* or Dee from Alice Walker's "Everyday Use." My existence was a complicated constriction where I brought my personal insecurities to a place and world that couldn't hold them, and, in fact, assigned them to an already-growing list of impediments they'd given me simply because I was Black.

As a result, I settled into that median. I was always hopeful but ever in despair. I was both happy and sad, up and down, over and under, back and forth. Being a Black woman who understood herself to be an empath—supersensitive to not just her own emotional experiences but also those of others—meant that there were tears always waiting to burst forth deep below but also a fiery rage that wanted to burn it all down. I am both/and, never either/or.

I was also a justice-oriented child. Which means that even though I chose to sit in that tension for as long as I did, I regularly felt the righteous pull toward freedom. Toward a firm stance of wholeness that didn't require anyone else's validation of my humanity. This sense of wanting things to be "right" came from feeling like the eight-year-old in me was left unprotected and therefore without justice. And now the forty-five-year-old me fiercely fights to validate my inner child.

It's human to want to be seen. We were created for connection and, I believe, our souls long for acceptance and acknowledgment. But it's a perversion of my humanity when I'm told that being seen by a particular group—White folks, in this case—is the only way I can have value and worth in this world. And this is the lie that Black people are taught to buy into from very early on. This notion that if my excellence is honored by the alleged standard-bearers then I'm worthy and if it isn't then I'm not can be catastrophic physically, emotionally, and spiritually. And having another Black or Brown face in the room can (but, sadly, doesn't always) ameliorate that damage. When Dr. McCoy-Deh stopped and said hi to me that day on campus, what transpired on the surface was, yes, the relief of seeing a face like mine. Certainly it was the opportunity for a new connection and friendship. But more than anything, it was the spark I needed to, for at least a moment, freely be myself. I'd been seen—but not in a way that forced me to talk, move, and think from the often-tenuous place of double consciousness.

People love to put us in a box. To say our joy should look like *this* or our anger should look like *that*. Part of the duality I *have* embraced is the fact that I rebuke and resist any categorization while vehemently claiming the categories, the identities, that align with my heart. I'm sure this feels confusing to some. *Do you want to be seen or not, Tracey? Do you want validation or not? Do you uphold the tenets of Black excellence or not? Does representation matter or not? Is double consciousness a good thing or not?*

My answer is: yes.

Remember . . . it's always both/and and never either/or.

People want to be able to definitively say *Tracey is this way* or *Tracey is this type of person*. In the same way, many White folks want to know what kind of Black person we are. They want to be able to name us because in naming us they are able to draw their conclusions and make their assumptions and feel pretty sure they are right about them both. But once again, this is a dehumanizing stance. It doesn't allow for the full range of emotions and actions available to us as human beings. And it's only with a more holistic lens we can truly be seen.

I had another experience with meeting a Black colleague on a different campus that wasn't exactly the same as that first encounter. Mostly because the climate was difficult, to say the least. By this point in my teaching career, I'd learned that there was a barely subconscious vetting process I needed to do when engaging with other Black folks on campus—that whole *all skinfolk ain't kinfolk* thing. I'd begun to get involved with quite a bit of diversity and inclusion work at the college and, along with other Black faculty members and White allies, had challenged the status quo that seemed to revere Whiteness and a subtly racist working environment. I'd watched this one woman in faculty meetings or other committee meetings from a distance, unsure of what her motivations were or whether or not she was the type of person whom I could connect with as a sister. I wanted to know what kind of kinfolk she would be. Whether she stood unapologetically in her Blackness and engaged with other Black folks on the job in a way that's meaningful, or if she was a climber, willing to step on anyone, especially those who look like her, to be the one at the top, the one who gave White folks the warm and fuzzies because she was willing to dance a jig.

Thankfully, Dr. Debonair Oates-Primus was the former. As I watched her expertly lead diversity and inclusion work on campus, I became intrigued but held my peace until I had the opportunity to see more.

It took me applying for an opportunity she was coordinating

to get a chance to engage with her and realize she was someone who could be trusted. I could talk about the experience of being Black in higher education and she not only could understand but also was willing to do whatever was necessary to break down the systems that made that a challenge. I not only had a chance to work alongside her to make radical changes in policy and culture on our campus; I also got to kick it with her at the annual Essence Festival in New Orleans (also known as Black girl heaven). I lucked out. Deb is a real one.

These kinds of engagements are so important. I needed to see myself in her in order to connect. Yes, my code-switching button is broken, but that doesn't mean I don't feel the pressure or the heat to conform. And it's always helpful to have someone else who gets you; who will ride for you.

Noticing a Black or Brown face in the room has always been about the potential for letting down my guard. My heart flips because there's the opportunity for joy. There is the chance for authenticity. Part of being human is doing the work to uncover both your identity and your divinity. You have to dig for it. Work for it. Wade through the many stories of life for it. Despite whatever traumas exist, when I'm able to embrace and then live my multi-dimensional self out loud, my heart overflows.

I do not want to downplay the emotional or spiritual injuries that make it challenging to allow our full selves to be seen while simultaneously understanding that we are inherently worthy. I've often been the one to feed these one-dimensional perspectives of myself to others. Mostly because I only feel safe enough to reveal one part of me. It's a way to protect myself. Allowing some parts to be seen could cause my endangerment. The problem with this, though, is that people will only respond to me according to the one part I show them.

Showing the breadth and depth of who we are and letting the chips fall where they may is the ultimate task of liberation. Sadly, we must normalize our humanity.

If they are not going to accept one of us, then let's make sure they don't accept any of us.

32

One Way Healing Comes

FOR WILLOW

She eyed me with both suspicion and hope. On the day we adopted her, I could tell she was wary of us. She hid under the Christmas tree on that first day. Made her preference for hard food and cardboard boxes known from jump. She seemed to be trying to figure out where'd she landed. Who were these people taking her from the only real home she'd ever known in her six months alive? I imagine the anticipation of a good life where she was loved and accepted, free to roam and explore, probably felt foreign.

We—and by "we" I mean "I"—also had reservations. We didn't know the circumstances of her birth. Where was she born? What had she seen? Did she experience any hardships in those six months? Would those hardships show up in bad behavior or nasty messes on my carpet born from her anxiety?

I didn't want a pet. Especially not a cat. I'd prejudged them. They just looked to me like they could turn our lives into a scene from *Pet Sematary* at any second. I imagined they thrived somewhere between evil and apathy. I especially didn't want a pet in the house. Just wasn't raised that way. Where I'm from, Black folks kept their pets outside. Which mostly meant they had dogs. A cat? No, ma'am. Plus, I'm a jumpy person. PTSD means I startle easy. So the idea of some creature suddenly sliding across my floor at random times or, as I would soon learn, having moments of pure insanity when they'd run across the room like a banshee did not sit well.

But our one-hundred-year-old house would not let us be great. The cracks and crevices, both seen and unseen, made it impossible to not have a mouser. And the one thing I hated more than animals who are pets was animals who aren't. My initial position was that the cat was only an employee. We brought her in to do a job. No hugs. No relationship beyond a professional one.

I would eventually learn that my resistance to pets, and in particular animals in the house, had a historical precedent. The relationship between Black folks and pets was way more intricate than I knew. Katheryn Lawson, a doctoral student at the University of Delaware at the time, wrote in her article "Pet Keeping and Pet Hiding in Black America": "The wide variety of decisions and experiences surrounding pet ownership in the black community reflect the many ways that they have negotiated with belonging and citizenship." Apparently, owning pets if one lived below the poverty line was problematic, especially if you accepted government assistance. Welfare recipients weren't allowed to own pets. In the mid- to late twentieth century, many people recounted trying to hide their pets in order to keep their benefits. Lawson writes:

The simple, and very human, act of keeping a dog as a companion, a friend and playmate . . . may be viewed as an act of resistance. Although pet keeping had become commonplace among middle-class households by the mid-1900s, those receiving welfare assistance were barred from sharing their homes with animals.

I suppose some might say this is a class issue. It likely is. But intersectionality—the concept developed by scholar Kimberlé Crenshaw, who highlights the interconnected nature of our various identities and how they are impacted by discrimination and bias—is a thing. Lawson goes on to discuss the problems specific to Black people: "In addition to legal obstacles to pet ownership, African-Americans have also been subject to a violent history in which dogs were enforcers of white supremacy and racial terror dating back to slavery." This makes sense to me. If the enslaved weren't allowed to have pets and post-Reconstruction through Jim Crow dogs, in particular, were used to terrorize and low-income people had to hide their pets while White, middle-class families freely treated their pets as members of the family, then pet ownership would inevitably be a complicated topic for some in our community. And still, during the Great Migration and afterward, many Black folks, aspiring to leave both the poverty and terror behind, also bought the lie that having pets within a particular—read: monied—context was respectable while having pets as someone who is poor was not:

Many middle-class African Americans counted animals among their family members and listed them alongside their education and committee service to prove their roles as respectable community leaders. Those who promoted the politics of respectability in the black community endorsed [these] white middle-class ideals in order to "elevate" their communities and gain respect from white America.

Even more interesting to me is what was lost to Black people when having a pet became so convoluted. There's been plenty of studies that show how pets, dogs and cats in particular, provide emotional support for individuals who suffer from post-traumatic stress disorder, PTSD. We now know that most African-Americans live with some form of racialized trauma, including transgenerational trauma like Post Traumatic Slave Syndrome (PTSS), a theory posited by scholar Joy DeGruy that "explains the etiology of many of the adaptive survival behaviors in African American communities throughout the United States and the Diaspora." So it would make sense that the denial of pets as a viable source of love, joy, and relief, or the positioning of pet ownership as solely a way to demonstrate a proximity to both wealth and Whiteness, was just another way to deny our humanity.

To be clear, though, I didn't know any of this when I scoffed at the idea of getting a house pet and later kept my distance from our cat. All I knew was that there was this adorable calico animal with fiery gold eyes waiting outside my bedroom every day and, well, whatever epigenetic baggage I carried, I needed to adjust to that.

And apparently she needed to adjust to me too. For months, we stared at each other. She'd purr and circle my feet curiously as I sat in our recliner chair. The same chair she'd leap into if my husband was sitting in it. Her meows were like cryptic messages that said, *I'm here. You're here. So what's good?*

Hidden behind her veil of feline mystery was fear, I suppose. Humans can be pretty freakin' scary. Some of us hold on to things until we have no more use for them. Until they can no longer serve us. Some of us have built a culture and civilization on individualism, and sentient beings beyond our immediate families are not held in light or love. And even the ones close to us can be disposable depending on our story. Depending on what has tainted our capacity for empathy and unconditional love.

I didn't see myself that way, though. I thought I had good reason for my disdain. I just didn't *do* animals. I wasn't terribly interested in starting to do them either. I was cool with my ambivalence. I didn't hate them but I didn't love them. Again, in my mind, she was hired for a job. My daughter and husband had more than enough love to give her. She didn't need mine.

So even despite her testing the waters with me, I stayed away. Of course I made sure she had food and water if my daughter forgot to fill her bowls—I'm not a monster. But I wasn't giving her my love.

Until I did.

The truth is, in that slick way of cats, she stole my love. Like a kitty pirate grifting her way into my consciousness, she demanded more than just the fulfillment of her basic needs. She wanted my attention. She soon moved on to rubbing her body against my leg whenever grief would show up on my face as tears. She sat guard next to me when my rage against one injustice or another sent me spiraling into harsh words and harsher feelings. The ultimate capture would occur almost a year to the day into her stay with us.

There are two places in our home Willow T. Cat—yes, that's her name—is not allowed. She knows better than to come into my bedroom or office. Those rooms are just off-limits for her. But one night my daughter wasn't feeling well. We heard her moaning in her bedroom about her stomach hurting. And in the age of COVID-19, those kinds of things are alarming. I mean, they're alarming regularly, but when you're in the middle of a pandemic you're always on heightened alert. Normally at night, the cat will sneak into my daughter's room and sleep on the edge of her bed or on the floor almost like she's standing guard. I always found that funny but never thought too much about it. On this day, my husband brought our daughter into our bedroom and as usual shut the door so the cat could not get in.

Meow.

Meow.

Meow, meow, meow, meow to infinity.

She's never liked when the three of us are in a room and she's not part of the mix. And since we'd taken away her roommate, she was not having it. It's almost as if she was saying, *Hey, look, you brought me here. Don't be trying to keep me out of the family business.* But we ignored her meows that night. We wanted to give our daughter some much-needed attention and allow her to get in the "big bed," as she would say, with Mommy and Daddy. So I gave her some things to help with her stomach- and headache and we all fell asleep.

Early the next morning, I got up to go to the restroom. Now, normally after making a fuss, Willow will eventually lie down in her bed and go to sleep. But because we'd taken her friend, her sister, into our bedroom, she was not about that life. As soon as I opened the door, she didn't do what she normally did, which was look at me funny and ascertain whether I'd finally give in and let her in the room. Nope, she did not care one bit about what I looked like. She shot past me and into the room like lightning.

Me: "Willow, get out of here! You don't belong here! You know better."

Willow: *Tuh*.

The cat lost her mind. She wildly ran to all four corners of the room looking for my daughter and then eventually jumped three feet onto the bed. She stood over my baby girl and stared at her as if to make sure she was okay.

"Get out of here, Willow!"

My daughter and husband started laughing uncontrollably. I guess I'm not the only one who plays zero games when it comes to that little girl. Once Willow realized that my daughter was fine, she left the room and then turned around and looked at me. I could have sworn I heard her meow, *Listen, I don't play about my people. So you're going to have to get over it.*

As angry as I was that she was in the room, I couldn't help but fall completely head over heels for her that day. There's something about protection that moves me. When you have grown up feeling like you were never protected, even watching a cat defend or protect a child will send you into such a sentimental space. Willow T. Cat is all right with me.

And no, I'm not *all the way* there yet. There are still days when I struggle with having an animal in the house. It's going to take some time to rewire that part of my brain. But her presence is, by far, not a nuisance anymore. It's actually welcome. And that is truly a miracle.

33

Joy with No Strings

There was a buzz in the air. Everyone around me was on pins and needles with excitement. Many felt like it was a turning point. Like there was really a possibility of shifting the election from what was clearly a path toward fascism. And when the media called the presidency for Joe Biden, there was so much rejoicing and even more relief. It was like there was this big collective exhale most people were savoring—except for me.

Have you ever watched people around you rejoice about something and while you feel happy and hopeful too, you can't fully settle into your own joy because you are waiting for things to go left? You are waiting for the proverbial other shoe to drop?

What I now know is this is very much the work of trauma. Sometimes when we experience trauma, what lodges in our body is what Brené Brown calls "foreboding joy." We learn to host "dress rehearsals for tragedy." We learn to prepare for the worst even when things are at their best. The ability to be fully present—and not be on high alert about what "might" or "could" happen—is stolen from us. For some of us, we've only survived by being experts at anticipating where the pain or harm will come next.

I was certainly glad that there was a shift from the road we were on, but I couldn't allow myself to get too happy about it. I did the obligatory posts of celebration, but I mostly scrolled my news feeds curious about the people who were so full of hope. Black and Brown folks were lauding Kamala Harris for being the first woman of color vice-president. And I get it. There was absolutely something to celebrate in that. I understood why people were just ready to move on from this botched experiment of blatant, invigorated White supremacy. Not that it didn't exist beforehand, but now it was on full display. Too many people who look like me had experienced horror at the hands of those who felt emboldened to come out of their flannel jackets or suit coats and enact violence at the bidding of the previous administration. Even if a new one only meant that White supremacy would simply take its next form, for many of us it was worth the risk.

But again, my life has taught me to be cautious with these things. And being this way means that, even beyond politics, it's hard to get superexcited about things that you actually should be enthusiastic about. When I think about the birth of my child, there was always an anxious joy hovering over every moment. Because I'd had two miscarriages and mine was considered a geriatric pregnancy at age thirty-six, my gynecologist would tell me, "Well, let's just get you to twenty-eight weeks." And when twenty-eight weeks came and went, she'd say, "Well, let's just get you to thirty-two weeks." Then, "Let's just get you to thirty-six weeks." It finally got to the point when I just said, "Okay, we're there. Chill out because you are making me really nervous." When my water broke at thirty-eight weeks, I was absolutely over the moon. And when she was born healthy, they laid her on my chest, and everything seemed okay. I could breathe now, right?

Maybe.

All I could think about was the fact that they were going to tell me I had to take this baby home. *I don't know how to be a mother!* There was so much anxiety. Sure, that's common. But there was so much wrapped up in my angst. *Some Black girls don't fare well in this world. And the ones who do seem to carry a boatload of bags to get to that place. I don't want that for my baby.* I couldn't sit fully in the joy of the moment because I was doubly overwhelmed. First with wondering if we'd drop her on the way out of the hospital. And second, if we'd drop her somewhere along the way to her adulthood.

I suppose that many people will say the answer to foreboding joy is to just push aside these feelings. Or ignore them. That never works, though. What I've learned is the best response is concession. The answer for me was to feel all the joy I possibly could, to fill my tank to full, so that when things shifted I could simply accept it knowing that joy was still accessible once that foreboding feeling passed. For the election, that meant dancing with my daughter—the one we have likely "dropped" a few times but who seems to still be growing wonderfully—as we watched Kamala Harris walk onto the stage to Mary J. Blige's "Work That" as she accepted her new position. Yes, the next day I felt the dread of all the problems that Harris and Biden were being challenged to fix. I knew the feeling was coming and accepted it. I sat with it knowing that another dance is possibly, maybe, I hope not too far off in the future.

For Black folks, our reality says that we shouldn't rejoice *too* much on Sunday because on Monday the overseer is waiting. We'd better not get *too* happy about getting the house we wanted in the neighborhood we wanted because somewhere around the corner a rock or a brick with "Nigger, get out" on it might be thrown through our perfect bay window. If we revel *too* much in the progress we are making for civil rights, then our leaders will be killed. If we delight *too* much in our ability to get into the schools we want, the positions we want, as high up the ladder as the Oval Office, there will be a Trump to arise from our triumph.

Here's the thing: there will always be pushback against our freedom; our liberation. We absolutely should expect it. But the beauty of our journey on this side of heaven is that we can live in two places at once. We can hold the tension of living fully in our joy, while accepting the moments when that joy shifts.

In order to respect but move out of our survival mode, and into a life of healing and wholeness, we must relearn how to be present. When foreboding joy shows up, we simply find our breath and be still. We anchor ourselves in the joy we know for sure, even when we know nothing else. No need to judge those foreboding thoughts. We don't even have to change them. We simply must think new ones. We create new neural pathways in our brain that say, *Hey, I can sit in my [insert emotion here], feel it completely, and still know joy.*

There is a Reiki healing principle that says: "Just for today, I will do my work honestly."

Just. For. Today.

The Christian Bible says: "Let tomorrow worry about itself" (Matthew 6:34).

I say: "All we really have is this moment . . . and this one. Honor it."

34

The Privilege of Wonder

Wonder pays no attention to priorities. . . .

—Durga Chew-Bose

I had to be about three or four. My mom was a single mother at the time, and we lived in a small two-bedroom apartment on Peabody Lane in Louisville. One of the things I loved to do was go outside and play. It's strange to consider this now. Living in a major metropolitan city like Philadelphia, I'm so clear that I would never let my three-year-old go outside and play on the sidewalk by herself or with another kid her age. I've been tainted by the knowledge of child trafficking and a very real sense that the world is maybe not as safe as it used to be.

But in the seventies, in Kentucky, this wasn't necessarily something a parent had to think about. I would go out on the little walkway in front of our home and play with my friend, A. A and her mother, my mom's friend L, lived at the very end of the block and we lived maybe halfway up it. Mine and A's favorite thing to do was ride our Big Wheels back and forth from her front door to mine.

Big Wheels weren't quite bikes. They were like low-seated tricycles made of plastic with a huge wheel in the front. Me and A's Big Wheels were very much an indication of our personalities. As much as I loved my tea set and dolls, I also loved to run, play, and flip. Back then I would have been called a tomboy. Whereas my friend was a bit more girly than me. At least that's how I remember her. Nevertheless, our Big Wheels said it all for us. She rode a pink Strawberry Shortcake Big Wheel and I, well, I rode a Dukes of Hazzard Big Wheel.

Yes. Dukes of Hazzard.

I was such a fan of those "good ol' boys" Bo and Luke Duke. Probably because the theme song was so catchy—I mean, I *was* three. I knew nothing about how problematic the show was. No one explained to me about the Confederate flag that was plastered across the top of the car. When the words of the song said "never meanin' no harm" I had no reason to believe otherwise.

Still. Picture a little Black girl in cornrows with beads and small pieces of aluminum foil at the ends riding a Dukes of Hazzard Big Wheel up and down the block. I'm sure it was a sight for woke eyes. But at the end of the day, I was with my best friend, doing this thing I loved to do, without a care in the world. Certainly without any awareness of the potential danger around me.

Despite the racism that clearly permeated most of the systems in my hometown, I lived in an area where people looked out for other people's children. My mom never said this, but I'm sure there might've been a neighbor or three who would see us playing and serve as an eyewitness if, God forbid, something were to happen to us. There was something incredible about being allowed to be free as a kid. To let your imagination to run wild. To sidestep the weight of the world before you can carry your own proverbial bags.

We hadn't yet been introduced to the terror.

I often wonder if that's what Tamir Rice felt in his last days. I wonder if, when he went outside that fateful day, all he could think about was playing cops and robbers or cowboys or ninjas or Superman or whatever else was on his mind. I wonder if he was just looking to be the FBI agent with the toy gun. I wonder if he thought he could run around the park and be a regular kid.

What Does It Mean to Be Regular for Black Kids Nowadays?

Just like me on my Big Wheel, maybe Tamir wasn't overly concerned about the potential of danger. Certainly he didn't believe that danger would come from an entity that was supposed to protect and serve regular kids playing in the park. I also wonder what Trayvon must've thought about being a regular kid, craving Skittles and a Snapple, talking to his friend on the way from the store and doing what teenagers do. Surely he didn't think a regular kid would have to protect himself from a danger he couldn't anticipate.

What Does It Mean for a Black Child to Be a Regular Kid and to Have Their Life Stolen from Them for Being Just That?

Black folks can be hard on our children. We are so conscious of the world in which they have to live, and we know that they don't always get to be regular. The freedom and imagination they have, like every child has, is limited very early on. We hand them fences and boundaries before they even get to play good. And as valid as our reasoning is, there's a price they pay for not having the privilege of wonder; for not getting to freely experience the joys of childhood.

I've had people offer their unsolicited opinions about my child's response to police officers. We were in a store one day and there was a cop just walking around, I guess doing what cops do. My daughter, who must have been five or six at the time, sees the man and runs behind my legs. She starts speaking in kid decibels, "Mommy, it's a po-po! Are they going to kill me? Are they going to kill us?"

In that moment, I felt like my heart was just going to burst. Like it would literally just beat itself right out of my chest.

This is not a result of me exposing her to too much. We don't watch the TV news or have it playing in the house. We were consistent in limiting screen time. But in light of the things I write about, I'm sure she had overheard conversations between me and my friends or me and her dad. I imagine in her six-year-old mind she was trying to piece it all together. Trying to figure out who is safe. Based on the evidence she gathered, the person with the badge was not.

It was different when I was a kindergartner. There was no social media. Conversations about the bad things were actively held in kitchen table convocations while I was playing elsewhere with other kids or took place in hushed whispers on corded phones. At school, they'd have the local police officer or fireman come in and talk to us about doing the right thing and making good choices. There was some attempt to protect our innocence even if it was under very false notions of respectability. What those police officers never said in the classroom was that as a Black person I can make all the right choices in the world, I can be minding my business, and if the wrong White person in authority doesn't honor my humanity in the same ways they might honor a White child's, then all that respectability flies out the window along with my safety—and my sense of wonder.

I want my child to be as free as any child on this planet. Not to have to concern herself that if she's doing the right thing, if she's having fun and not breaking the law, somehow she could still be harmed. But I can't say that to her yet. What I can do is help her figure out how, if being a regular kid is not an option, to experience joy alongside of or within the reality of the world she lives in. I can be gentle with her because I know the price of wonder is too great. I can do what Black parents have been trying to do for generations. Set boundaries but also build emotional and physical shelters. Create literal spaces for our children—the ones we birthed and the ones under our gaze—to have peace and joy and all the wonder of other regular kids. Some of us have more resources than others to be able to do that, and that alone speaks to the systemic issues that keep beating us in the head whenever we try to make space for our humanity. But to restore ourselves, we have to keep trying. For our babies' sake and our own, we must hold fast to our wonder.

35

Time and Intention

After our sixteen years together, I'm sure there are many things that drive my husband crazy about me. But the one thing I know makes him want to pull out his nonexistent hair (he's bald) is the fact that I believe that I can go or be anywhere in fifteen minutes. Never mind that an event is thirty miles away or there's six feet of snow or it's rush hour and traffic is a beast or I left the house five minutes *after* I was supposed to arrive. All of that is inconsequential. If you ask me how long it's going to take me to be anywhere, I'm going to say, "Oh, about fifteen minutes." And every time, I know he wants to scream.

Sorry, not sorry. Fifteen minutes always sounds like a reasonable time to get someplace. Anything more than that and it feels like it will take too long, and I don't want to think about it. Anything less than that and, well, that's just plain dumb.

Our conversations usually go a little like this:

Him: "Hey, babe, what time do you need to be on campus?"

Me: "Oh, at about nine thirty."

Him: "Okay, it's nine. You better get going."

Me: "Nah, I still got about fifteen minutes before I have to leave."

Insert eye roll, headshake, and, if I look closely, probably smoke coming out of his ears.

Him: "You do know there's going to be traffic along Kelly Drive."

Me: "Yes."

Him: "And you do know it takes thirty minutes to get to your campus on a good day."

So you say. . . .

Before you ask, I don't know why I'm like this. I've lived in major cities all my adult life. Cities like Chicago, New York, and Philly. It has never taken me only fifteen minutes to get anywhere except maybe around the block.

I often wonder if this is a kind of protective stance. A way of holding control or power. Whatever it is, it usually ends with me being frustrated. And, of course, late.

I've always been very curious about the way humans mark time. Why exactly does one sunset and sunrise equal a day? Why not have forty-eight-hour days with frequent long naps as the norm? I'm sure that the earliest, agrarian versions of us were well intentioned in needing mornings to begin at one time and evenings to begin at another, but why is it necessary to still uphold those conventions?

According to Sunday Funmilola Babalola and Olusegun Ayodeji Alokan, PhD, in the paper "African Concept of Time, a Socio-Cultural Reality in the Process of Change," written for the *Journal of Education and Practice*:

Africans [sic] ideas of time are highly philosophical. Time to them is beyond the natural socio-cultural phenomena. It is also understood in its ontological conception. [John] Mbiti has effectively used the Swahili word Zamani to describe the stretches of time into timeless eternity. The Yoruba people also see time beyond what is experienced physically. It stretches to the period of the life after death, the realm of the ancestors. . . .

Zamani, in Mbiti's conception, is not limited to what in English is called the past. In African ontology, it has its own "past" "present" and "future," but on a wider scale. We can, for the sake of convenience, call it the macro time.

Our ancestors' understanding of time, when separated from the influence of colonization and Westernization, feels way more expansive. If Black peoples around the world were to return to a three-dimensional, 360-degree view of time, particularly in relation to how we move through the world, I suspect that our notions of what is important to do in any given moment would change also.

I do know that shifting the way we see time is directly linked to the way we view and ultimately process joy. A common refrain I've heard by many in the Black community when one starts to talk about resting and wellness strategies is the emphatic, "Ain't nobody got time for that." But what happens when we can make time for the very things that will hold us together? If we name our time according to the joys we want to experience in it? I'm clear that joy exists in and among us without having to name it. Most of us recognize the raucous laughter of a multi-generational round of the Electric Slide or Wobble. But there's also power in naming our joy, in being intentional about giving joy a specific time and designated space in order to help us heal. There's freedom in being able to choose what joy looks like.

Children offer us the best demonstrations of what it means to set aside time for joy or, using African concepts, weaving time for joy throughout the fullness of our days. Finding fun is what kids do. They may have chores and schoolwork to do. If they're teenagers, they might even have a job. Unlike adults, though, most of their lives are not centered on the work they have to do. At least they shouldn't be. Most children are always actively looking for ways to experience joy.

Every month or so, my husband and I will set up special one-on-one days or weekends with our daughter. She loves our mommy-daughter or daddy-daughter dates. She so looks forward to them that she makes an extensive plan. In one of her twelve diaries, she writes a list of all the things she wants to do:

Make pancakes or waffles with bananas and berries on top.
Watch the Tinkerbell movie.
Go to the park and ride bikes.
Snuggle time.

She's very meticulous about her plan to have a good time. Yes, she might still have to wash the dishes or finish her math worksheets, but those are rarely front and center. It's not even likely they will make the list. In her mind, those are just the things she has to do. They're not the center of her experience for the day. The kid sets her mind and thoughts around her intentions to engage joy.

I wonder how our lives would change if we approached our days like my nine-year-old. Yes, we have to go to work. Yes, we have to take care of the kids. Yes, we have 50 million other necessary things we have to do during our days. But what if those things only served as the background to things we are really focused on? What if we planned for all our joy moments? Made a list of all the things we plan to do in a day that will bring us joy and serve our souls? So we know we have to drop our child off at school, but what if we write in singing the latest Beyoncé girl power anthem at the top of our lungs along the way?

There must be a way we can write in our joy so that we don't spiral into productivity hell. Our restoration as individuals and a collective means we don't want to look up one day and realize we cannot recall the last time we laughed or smiled. In a season when the news is steadily punching us in the gut with all kinds of terror, we have to write our joy in.

I may not be able to overhaul the way humanity has chosen to mark time. But if my healing and liberty depend on me taking control over how I divvy out my own minutes and hours, then I will choose twelve or eight or three—whatever I can grasp— hours of joy a day forever and ever, amen.

36

What Freedom Looks Like on Her

Is there anything more beautiful than a woman set free?
no longer barely grasping at destiny
but cradling it in her arms
rocking it back and forth to the beat of her heart
made full by love and joy and peace and
the release of pains known and lost.

the rhythm, simple and complex
—at the same time
understood and mysterious
—at the same time.

There is nothing . . .
no graven image,
no circumstance,
that surpasses the sovereignty of God
and the woman who has surrendered to it.

I remember sitting at the river one day and seeing a couple who looked very comfortable with each other moving along the stone pathway. The fascinating thing was they were side by side, but one of them was walking and the other was jogging. It didn't appear to be intentional. For the one running, there was obvious exertion. And it seemed like the one who was walking just didn't *need* to run in order to maintain the pace of the one who was jogging. Nevertheless, they were moving toward their destination, each in their own way and at their own pace.

Nowadays, we are constantly inundated with the play-by-plays of our faves' lives. Everyone has an opinion and believes it's worth sharing. As a writer, I find it's a slippery slope writing about Black joy and all the ways Black folks show it, live it, or desire more of it. But even then, my stories, my observations, are just that—mine. I'm desperate for my people to heal in all the ways we need to, but I never want anyone to determine the pace of their lives—how fast or slow they move toward joy and healing—by the pace of me or anyone else. Because here's the raw truth: our pace will always look different from that of those around us—even those we think are right along beside us.

The liberation of Black people, inclusive of our Black bodies, minds, and spirits, is an interesting case study on the relationship between the personal and the political, the individual and the collective. We are so connected. For the sake of our freedom, my joy is very much connected to the next Black person's, and so on. We are all moving toward the destination of liberty, but we are not—nor do we have to be—moving at the same pace. Just like those two people walking/running along the river, some of us may only need to stroll leisurely toward embracing our joy fully and completely while someone else might need to run with intensity, exert more energy, to get to that same place.

That's okay. I think the larger, more significant question we all have to ask ourselves is this: Is it worth running to keep up? I think the answer is yes. No, we don't want to exhaust ourselves trying to do what someone else is doing in the same way. We don't need to rock out at a pace that's not suitable for us individually. But if there must be a goal of Black joy, then it's Black freedom, and the only requirement is that we keep moving and we arrive together.

My personal definition of freedom is simply doing the next right thing to heal—for my own well-being and that of my child. But what does that look like for the collective? How does my individual experience serve a non-monolithic group of people who have different ideas on what the next right thing is? It at least begins with an exploration and understanding of our own context. What is the context of our pain and suffering at the hands of White supremacy? What joy has come out of our experience that serves us and what residue should be trashed forever? And the crux of it all: Are we desperate enough for liberation that we are willing to reach out for it without asking for permission or running it by people who don't have our collective mental, physical, and spiritual healing in mind?

When my time comes, I want to die empty. Not empty as in having a huge void. More like knowing that I pursued and maybe even accomplished every dream I'd ever dreamt. That I've fulfilled every purpose assigned by my God. That I've given away every gift I had to be used and replicated for future generations. That I've left a full legacy to be poured out by others again and again.

What Does Freedom Look Like on Her?

It looks like arriving at the end of my life only carrying the work I've done and the joy and peace I allowed myself to have. For some of us, we will arrive empty-handed because we chose to forgo joy not only for ourselves but also for those around us. Others of us will arrive with bags we'll never be able to carry into our afterlife. We're weighted down with anger and despair, sometimes even rightfully so. Shame sits on our spines like a hiking backpack, hard and stiff, upright and unbending, and having unnaturally slowed our pace.

None of us are immune to this, by the way. We only have control over whether we release it or not. Generation after generation we all seem destined to pick up the pain of our mothers and fathers, our culture and communities, and carry it forward even in the midst of our progress. And it's in that carrying that I wonder if we lose a little bit of who we inherently are. Our connection to the great Mystery—what I call God—can be lost. We are burdened with other people's stuff. Sometimes even in utero. Some of us are born heavy.

But as writer Kiese Laymon writes in his memoir, *Heavy*, being heavy doesn't have to prevent us from flying. I certainly hope this is true. I know that Toni Morrison wrote in *Song of Solomon*: "You wanna fly, you got to give up the shit that weighs you down." I think the work of every human is to release as much of that weight as we can. But for those of us who can't, I hope that we can still find a way to fly. In fact, maybe that's what Black joy is at its core. Finding a way to fly even if it's just our souls that can take flight.

What Does Freedom Look Like on Us?

It looks like a deep well of love and compassion in our souls. A gushing overflow of desire that seeks peace and joy for ourselves but also others in our community. And the most amazing thing is, as free people, we are not afraid to dig for it. We aren't afraid of taking the metaphorical shovel of contemplation and reflection and tearing away at the dirt and sediment of White supremacy that has tried to bury us. Some things in our lives die and stay dead. Other things die only to be resurrected better and stronger. The key to living well and with joy is knowing the difference between the two.

I'm so proud of the way Black people have reinvented what life has delivered to us. That is our gift. We are alchemists. Transforming, seemingly by magic, a hard thing into something valuable and useful and, yes, filled to overflowing with joy.

Acknowledgments

I am grateful for the Holy Spirit who infuses my life with joy and grace even when I can't see it. Even when I don't want to see it. I forever yield to Your guidance and direction.

I am grateful for my beautiful mother and the books and magazines she kept around the house my entire childhood. I remember being barely eight years old and sneaking to read Toni Morrison's *Song of Solomon* and *Essence* magazines when I clearly had no business doing so. Oh, well! I guess it paid off. That normalization of reading and storytelling laid the foundation for my love of words and this life of purpose I now have. I love you more.

I am grateful for my parents who, in your own way, made room and space for my gifts. I imagine that some of what you read here is hard. And yet, I know that you know there is room for my truth; for all our truths.

I am grateful for the community of writers who have gone before me; my literary ancestors—Toni Morrison, Zora Neale Hurston, James Baldwin, Audre Lorde, Toni Cade Bambara, and so, so many more.

I am grateful for the community of writers who stand alongside me. Too many to name but who, as Black church folks love to say, "thought it not robbery" to support and challenge and love on me and my work.

I am grateful for my community of family and friends—also too many to name—who choose to walk this life out with me; who know I will always "do the most" and don't mind it one bit.

Many, many thanks to my agent, Cait Hoyt of Creative Artists Agency, for believing in me. For taking a chance on a relatively unknown writer and seeing what my work and words could be and do in this world. Also, much love and gratitude to Madeleine Morel at 2M Communications, for telling the publishing world about this one writer in Philly. Both of you have put my name in rooms I could have never imagined before.

Thank you so much to Karyn Marcus, Rebecca Strobel, Awura Ama Barnie-Duah, and the whole Gallery Books/Simon & Schuster team. It's been such a wonderful experience taking this journey with you. Thank you, Kate Dresser, who saw the value in these stories and leaped at the chance to help put them out into the world. Forever grateful.

To the loves of my life:

William, thank you for your unwavering support. My dreams have always been safe with you. For all the days and nights you watched me unravel while writing this book and told me that it would be alright. You were right. I love you.

To MaKayla, my sweet, fierce sugarplum: Every day I look at you and see so much freedom and joy and authenticity. You dance to the beat of your own drum and see life as yours for the living. I have made it my mission to do whatever I can to ensure that this world doesn't steal any of that from you. Like the song you just wrote the day before I'm writing this, you are "beau-

tiful and bright, [you are] Black, Black, so Black, that's right!"
That's right, Baby.

I will forever be humbled by the doors that have opened for me, but also by the ones that have closed. Both have been a testament to my willingness to work hard but, more than anything, to a deep down, ever-present understanding that I am worthy. Period.

About the Author

As a writer and educator, **Tracey Michae'l Lewis-Giggetts** offers those who read her work and hear her speak an authentic experience: an opportunity to explore the intersection of culture, identity, and faith/spirituality at the deepest levels. She is the founder of HeARTspace, a healing community created to serve those who have experienced trauma of any kind through the use of storytelling and the arts.

Tracey has published sixteen books including several collaborations with numerous high-profile authors. In 2016, Tracey was honored by SheKnows Media as one of the "Voices of the Year" for her nuanced and personal exploration of mental health, PTSD, and self-care. In 2021, Tracey became one of twenty writers who contributed to the groundbreaking book *You Are Your Best Thing: Vulnerability, Shame Resilience, and the Black Experience* edited by the founder of the MeToo Movement, Tarana Burke, and acclaimed researcher Brené Brown.

Tracey has spoken on a number of platforms around the country on topics related to race/social justice, healing, and faith/spirituality. Additionally, Tracey's freelance work has been published in print and online publications such as *O, The Oprah Magazine, The Washington Post, Essence, The Guardian, The Chronicle of Higher Education, Ebony Magazine,* TheRoot.com, and more.